MEN-AT-ARMS SERIES

EDITOR: MARTIN WINDROW

W9-AXS-417

American Civil War Armies (1): Confederate

Artillery, Cavalry and Infantry

Text by PHILIP KATCHER

Colour plates by RON VOLSTAD

OSPREY PUBLISHING LONDON

Published in 1986 by
Osprey Publishing Ltd,
59 Grosvenor Street, London, W1X 9DA
© Copyright 1986 Osprey Publishing Ltd
Reprinted 1987 (three times), 1988, 1989, 1990

British Library Cataloguing in Publication Data

Katcher, Philip
    American Civil War armies.—(Men-at-arms; 170)
    1: Confederate artillery, cavalry and infantry
    1. Confederate States of America *Army*—Equipment
    2. Confederate States of America *Army*—Uniforms
    3. United States—History—Civil War 1861–1865
    —Equipment and supplies
    I. Title   II. Series
    355.8′0973   UC86

    ISBN 0-85045-679-7

Filmset in Great Britain
Printed in Hong Kong

Artist's Note

Readers may care to note that the original paintings
from which the colour plates in this book were
prepared are available for private sale. All
reproduction copyright whatsoever is retained by the
publisher. All enquiries should be addressed to:
    Ronald B. Volstad
    PO Box 1577
    Main Post Office
    Edmonton
    Alberta
    Canada T5J 2N9
The publishers regret that they can enter into no
correspondence upon this matter.

Author's Note

This title covers the uniforms, arms and personal
equipment issued by the national Confederate
government to its artillery, cavalry, and infantry.
These units, for the most part, bore state designations,
e.g., the 10th Virginia Volunteer Infantry Regiment
which was, despite the title, supplied by the
Confederate government. At the same time some
states, such as North Carolina and Florida, outfitted
many of their troops themselves, and sometimes had
their own uniform regulations. Moreover, most states
maintained some form of state forces, military and
naval, for local defence. These state-supplied units will
be covered in a future title devoted to the state forces
of the Civil War, both Northern and Southern.

Introduction

When the Southern states seceded from the United States to form their own government in 1861, one of their first moves was to organise an army for their defence. It was made up initially of volunteers, many of whom had already served in pre-war volunteer companies. Conscription laws were introduced in 1862, although with many loopholes (including an exemption for newspaper editors!) Most of the South's 500,000 fighting men were young, from rural, farming backgrounds. They served from the time of their enlistment until the end of the war, receiving $11 a month (for a private) in inflated currency, poor rations, and even worse clothing—and this despite the fact that one of the first steps taken by the new army was to design a uniform and establish standards for accoutrements and weapons.

As most of the high-ranking officers came from the US Army, it is not surprising that the basic influence on Confederate Army practices was the 'old' army of the Mexican–American War of 1846–48. In the field the enlisted men wore short jackets with standing collars and a single row of buttons, plain trousers, and a peaked forage cap. For 'dress' they wore frock coats and shakos. Officers wore frock coats, although many mounted officers also wore short jackets. The system of non-commissioned rank insignia, the grades themselves, and branch-of-service colours were also adopted from the most recent US Army regulations.

There were also a number of foreign influences on the adopted Confederate dress. From the army of

The Confederate infantryman as he appeared in the field. His cap is a grey 'chasseur' pattern; his wool shirt, trousers and jacket are also dark grey. His brass buttons are marked 'I'; his canteen is a captured US Army model covered in grey wool; his blanket is tan with a black stripe near the end; his weapon is a Richmond-made rifled musket; and his cast 'CS' rectangular beltplate is the type worn by Western Confederates, rather than men of the Army of Northern Virginia. (Smithsonian Institution)

This drawing, done by a Confederate veteran and entitled 'On the Confederate line of battle "with fate against them"' gives a good indication of the ragged, non-uniform appearance and loose tactical formations of the Confederate infantry in action. (*Battles & Leaders of the Civil War*)

Imperial France, then considered the best in the world by many overseas observers impressed by Louis Napoleon's campaigns in Africa, the Crimea and Italy, came the cap styles, and the officers' insignia worn on the caps and sleeves—the 'Austrian knot'. There is some evidence that the basic uniform design itself was adapted from that of the Austrian Army, which at the time wore double-breasted, greyish-white tunics with facing-colour collars (on which officers' insignia was worn), sky-blue trousers, and French-type caps—in some ways very similar to regulation Confederate dress.

The regulations issued by the Confederate Army on 6 June 1861 called for quite a smartly turned-out soldier. In practice, however, the actual fighting officer or man of the artillery, cavalry or infantry was rarely a fashion plate. In part this was due to the South's lack of manufacturing facilities at home, and of financial resources to buy uniforms, accoutrements and weapons abroad in sufficient numbers for all its men. In part it was also due to the naturally independent spirit of Southern men, who would rather wear what they fancied than what was ordered.

This is not to say that the Confederate soldier was always ragged or badly equipped. In fact, the average officer or enlisted man appears generally to have been issued virtually everything he needed. In early 1865 Confederate Quartermaster Maj. William Cross wrote that the men received 'a fair provision in all articles save overcoats and flannel jackets, and in some instances an extravagant consumption [was made]. The condition of the troops in comparison with the issues made suggests either an imperfect distribution of supplies, or waste on the part of the individual soldier, or it may be both. The latter is known to prevail to an extent that makes it a great abuse.'

In fact, the Quartermaster Department clearly issued clothing more frequently than regulations called for. According to regulations, each soldier would receive two jackets in his first year of service and one a year thereafter. He would also receive three pairs of trousers the first year and two a year thereafter. Quartermaster General A. R. Lawton reported on 27 January 1865 that, 'This Department has never aimed to limit its issues to this standard, especially in regard to jackets and pants, but has endeavored to provide a suit of clothing every six months for each man.'

Figures tend to confirm these statements. Although the Army of Northern Virginia is generally described as ragged—and this agrees with photographs taken of dead of this army—between 1 October 1864 and 21 January 1865 the Army's troops were issued 104,199 jackets, 140,578 trousers, 167,862 pairs of shoes, 74,851 blankets, 27,011 hats and caps, 21,063 flannel shirts, 157,727 cotton shirts, 170,138 pairs of drawers, 146,136 pairs of socks, and 4,861 overcoats. During this time the Army's average strength at Petersburg and Richmond was 49,521. Clearly, excepting only overcoats, there should have been enough for all.

It should be noted that one soldier reckoned that the average pair of trousers was worn out by a soldier in the field within a month, and that a jacket would last only three. Therefore, despite generous issues, there would have been times when many Confederates in the field would have been ragged indeed.

Even so, the average Confederate infantryman had a hat, several shirts, a jacket, underclothing, a pair of trousers, several pairs of socks, and a pair of shoes. (A British observer also noted that it was a common practice in the Army of Northern Virginia to stick a tooth brush in a buttonhole on the jacket front.) The jacket and trousers were supposed to have been made of wool, regardless of the season. This was regretted by some veterans, who would have liked to have had summer-weight cotton uniforms issued. Indeed, in 1865 the Quartermaster Department's Maj. Cross wrote: 'By using cotton clothing during the summer and spring, and reserving the woollen goods for fall and winter, it is hoped and believed that enough may be had to prevent suffering next winter.' This suggests that some cotton uniforms were indeed issued. It is certain that many of the uniforms were made of a wool/cotton mixture that was lighter in weight than all-wool uniforms.

The infantryman's accoutrements included a waist belt; a small leather pouch worn on his right front hip, containing copper percussion caps; a

An oil-cloth rain cover is worn on the forage cap of this soldier from Ashville, North Carolina. The large bow-tie would not last long in the field. His grey frock coat has coloured tape trimming around the standing collar and on each cuff. (Lee Joyner)

larger leather pouch for cartridges, worn either on its own sling from left shoulder to right hip or on his waist belt; a leather scabbard for the iron and steel bayonet, worn on his left hip; a canvas haversack for provisions, worn from his right shoulder to his left hip; and a water-bottle over that. Several men in a company might also carry some cooking gear such as frying pans or pots slung from their shoulders. A blanket roll worn slung from left shoulder to right hip completed the accoutrements. His weapon was a 0.577 or 0.58 in. calibre rifled musket. Fourth Texas Infantry Pte. J. B. Polley reckoned that this load 'was never less than thirty-six pounds, and often went a little beyond forty'.

There were, of course, extremes at both ends of the scale. A Union soldier described finding a dead Confederate infantryman armed with an Enfield and carrying a British-made cartridge box: 'Ragged trousers, a jacket, a shirt of what used to be

Capt. James Tucker, 9th Florida Infantry, wears a regulation infantry officer's coat with sky-blue collar and cuffs. He holds his broad-brimmed slouch hat. His buttons appear to be of the state pattern, which bore the design of a six-pointed star within a wreath over the word FLORIDA. (Fritz Kirsch)

"tow cloth", a straw hat which had lost a large portion of both crown and brim, completed his attire. . . A haversack hung from his shoulder. Its contents were a jack knife, a plug of twisted tobacco, a tin cup, and about two quarts of coarsely cracked corn with, perhaps, an ounce of salt, tied in a rag. . . This was a complete inventory of the belongings of one Confederate soldier.'

On the other hand, a soldier named Tennessee Thompson in the 1st Tennessee Infantry Regiment was said to carry more 'than any other five men in the army', a fellow veteran recalled: 'For example, he carried two quilts, three blankets, one gum oil cloth, one overcoat, one axe, one hatchet, one camp-kettle, one oven and lid, one coffee pot, besides his knapsack, haversack, canteen, gun,

cartridge-box, and three days' rations.'

The artilleryman's uniform was generally the same, but his accoutrements comprised only the haversack and water-bottle with, sometimes, a waist belt with a holster for a revolver on his left hip, a cap pouch, and a pistol cartridge box which was, in size, between the cap pouch and musket cartridge box. He generally discarded his issue sabre. The cavalryman had the same waist belt with leather pouches, holster, and a scabbarded sabre hung from slings on his left hip. He also wore a wider leather sling from left shoulder to right hip with a large iron spring-hook to which his carbine was clipped.

Officers wore the same sword belts, holsters with pistols and ammunition, and cap pouches. Foot officers also usually carried haversacks and canteens, with a small knapsack or blanket roll in the field. Wrote one of them: 'I have my sword, a blanket, haversack, canteen, and a change of under-clothing in a light knapsack, and let everything else go; for our wagons are always far off—you never can find what you put in them—and as we are continually moving about, I find my load sufficiently heavy without adding to it. When ordered to march, I am at the head of my company, heavily laden as any; the boy makes a fire when the halt is sounded, and throwing myself down on my blanket, I share my rations with some "mess" or other, and am ready to move or fight at a moment's notice. As to thinking of toilet and appearance, a full supply of pots and pans for cooking, it is all nonsense. Our wagons are scarcely sufficient to carry tents, ammunition and flour.'

So equipped, the fighting Confederate was ready for action.

Headgear

The Confederate War Department ordered on 19 April 1861 that forage caps (no colour given) would be issued to members of its regular army. On 6 June 1861 this was elaborated, and the caps were described as being similar to French képis, with branch-of-service coloured pompons worn in front—red for artillery, light blue for infantry, and yellow for cavalry. On 24 January 1862 this was revised; the pompons disappeared, and henceforward the caps were to have dark blue bands, with sides and crowns in branch-of-service colours.

Moreover, the caps were to have markings that would indicate commissioned ranks: three gold stripes on the front, back, and sides for field officers, two for captains, and one for lieutenants. The same number of gold braids were to form a quatrefoil knot on the crown of the cap. Enlisted men were to wear their regimental numbers on the cap front. White duck or linen 'havelocks'—sun covers like those popularly associated with the French Foreign Legion—were to be worn in summer, and oil-cloth covers in bad weather, according to an order issued 24 January 1862. Neither of these two items seem to have been worn in any great numbers after the very early months of the war.

Such caps as were worn appear to have differed from the regulations. Many had peaks made of cardboard covered with black-painted cloth, and black-painted cloth sweatbands. One such cap, worn by an enlisted man in the Richmond Howitzers, had dark blue-grey wool sides and a red cotton/wool mixed band and crown. Grey caps with

branch-of-service coloured bands appear to have been fairly common; even more so were plain grey caps. A 4th Texas Infantry Regiment private even recalled making his own cap out of a woollen shirt, with a peak made from a 'generous slice of stirrup leather'.

According to Army of Northern Virginia veteran Frank H. Foote, 'Our hats and caps were taken from "our friends, the enemy", and you could see all styles, shapes and makes, generally ornamented with letters denoting the command of the owner. The "alpine hat" or "Excelsior" of New York was the most common, and was preferred to all others. Caps were not sought after, as they neither turned sun nor rain. Slouch hats are peculiar to the South, and were affected a great deal. We also had palmetto, pine straw and quilted cloth hats.'

Indeed, most veterans agreed that caps were not the preferred field wear. A study of photographs of

The official tailor's plate from the Confederate Army's dress regulations as published in 1862. It shows the different pieces of woollen cloth used in making the frock coat. The jacket was cut the same way, with the skirts omitted.

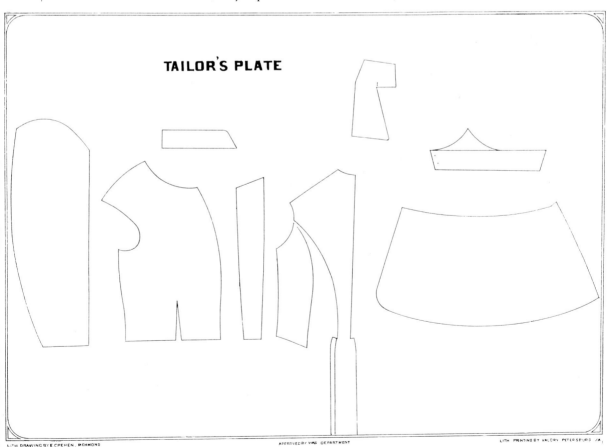

TAILOR'S PLATE

LITH DRAWING BY E CREHEN . RICHMOND   APPROVED BY WAR DEPARTMENT   LITH. PRINTING BY VALORY. PETERSBURG VA

Confederate enlisted men in the field taken after 1862 indicated that out of 225 men who could be seen clearly enough to reveal the type of hat being worn, only 26 per cent wore peaked caps. The rest wore the preferred slouch hats. Of those in slouch hats, 59 per cent wore light-coloured hats, either tan or grey, while the rest were dark, either black or dark brown.

Surviving soldiers' hats have brims between $2\frac{3}{4}$ ins. and 4 ins. wide, with a narrow silk ribbon running around the band. A typical one in the

Museum of the Confederacy has a $4\frac{1}{2}$ in.-tall crown. Straw hats, old or copied US Army M1839 forage caps, captured Union Army hats, and all manner of civilian hats were also worn.

Most hats were apparently worn without badges or cords, though two officers' hats in the Confederate Museum have US Army-type hat cords. Orders called for a regimental number to be worn, however, and it does appear that many men did wear some sort of regimental cap badge. One soldier was photographed in May 1864 wearing a slouch hat turned up with a white badge marked 'Al 4', suggesting the 4th Alabama Infantry Regiment, which did serve in the area where the photograph was made. Other sources noted seeing soldiers

Starke's Brigade of Louisiana troops, out of ammunition, holds off Federal troops with stones at Second Manassas, 1862. Note the short jacket worn by the officer on the bottom right. (*Battles & Leaders of the Civil War*)

wearing the insignia of the 18th and 21st Georgia Infantry Regiments and the 11th North Carolina Infantry Regiment, apparently in some form of hat badges.

At least one officer was photographed wearing a cap badge of the letters 'CSA' within a laurel wreath. Other officer photographs show US Army officers' branch-of-service cap badges being worn; this practice, however, was not common.

Another fashion of 1861 was the wearing of blue 'secession cockades' on hats. In 1862 a soldier in Kentucky 'saw what I had long forgotten—a "cockade". The Kentucky girls made cockades for us, and almost every soldier had one pinned on his hat.' These cockades were also often worn on the left breast of the coat.

Coats

Officers' Coats
On 6 June 1861 General Order Number Four was issued. By its terms all officers were ordered to wear cadet grey double-breasted tunics, 'the skirt to extend halfway between the hip and the knee'. There were to be four buttons on the back and skirt of the tunic, the hip buttons on a line with the lowest breast buttons. Cuffs were to be fastened with three small buttons, and there were to be seven buttons in each row on the front. The collar was to be standing, with embroidered rank insignia—one, two or three $\frac{1}{2}$ in. gold bars, the top one 3 ins. long, for a second lieutenant, first lieutenant and captain respectively; and one, two or three $1\frac{1}{4}$ in. gold stars for a major, lieutenant-colonel and colonel respectively. There was also to be an Austrian knot in gold braid—one braid for lieutenants, two for captains, and three for field officers—above the pointed cuff on each sleeve. Cuffs and collars were to be in branch-of-service colours. Because these insignia made the officers stand out as good targets, on 3 June 1862 orders were issued allowing officers to dispense with collar insignia when wearing fatigue dress in the field. A 1st Tennessee Infantry Regiment veteran recalled that this was a common practice in his regiment in late 1861, even before this order was issued.

At first many officers also wore US Army officers'

Note the trimming, probably yellow, and the two buttons placed as decoration on the collar of this otherwise plain jacket worn by Private Bentley Weston, 7th South Carolina Cavalry Regiment. (Library of Congress)

shoulder straps, and as late as 21 March 1862 the Richmond *Daily Dispatch* newspaper warned officers against this practice.

As officers bought their own uniforms, most conformed to regulations; but there were a number of variations. Many simply wore a single row of buttons—as the Union naval blockade grew tighter, brass buttons became quite expensive. Other officers had their coats made entirely of grey, without the facings in branch-of-service colours. Some had collars made lay-down style, in the fashion of contemporary civilian frock coats, with rank insignia embroidered on the top of them. And mounted officers often wore waist-length jackets, called 'roundabouts'. These appeared either with or without branch-of-service colours, with one or two rows of buttons, and with or without Austrian knots.

Another variation of officer's tunic was the 'sack

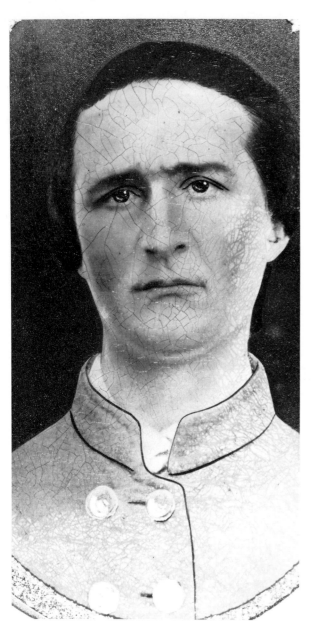

A second row of buttons appears to have been added by an artist to this soldier's single-breasted coat. The subject is Private Andrew Jackson Rodgers of Company A, 27th Georgia Infantry Regiment. The 27th, part of Maj.Gen. D. H. Hill's Division, lost 104 officers and men defending their position along a turnpike during the Battle of Antietam, 17 September, 1862. (Lee Joyner)

Enlisted Men's Coats

On 19 April 1861 the War Department authorised the issue of dark blue smocks 'worn as a blouse' as its issue enlisted men's dress. This was changed on 6 June 1861, when enlisted men were given a regulation coat resembling that worn by officers save that it lacked the Austrian knots; had only two small buttons on each cuff; lacked buttons on the rear of the coat; and had no insignia on the collar. Collars and cuffs were to be in branch-of-service colours.

Non-commissioned grade was to be marked by branch-of-service colour chevrons worn points down. These included two chevrons for corporal; three for sergeant; three with a diamond in the angle for first or orderly sergeant; three chevrons and three straight bars for quartermaster sergeant; three chevrons and a star for ordnance sergeant; and three chevrons and three arcs for sergeant major. Some time in 1863 US Army company quartermaster sergeants started wearing three chevrons and a single bar, and this insignia also appears to have been adopted by some Confederate company quartermaster sergeants. (A number of unexplained chevrons or sleeve badges also appear in original photographs; one cavalryman was even photographed, intriguingly, with an apparently yellow prancing horse decorating each sleeve where chevrons would usually appear.)

A study made of photographs showing Confederates in the field suggests that not all those authorised to wear chevrons did so—only two corporals out of hundreds of photographed men wear chevrons, while a similar sample of US soldiers generally includes a much larger proportion of non-commissioned officers wearing chevrons. One veteran of the 1st Tennessee Infantry Regiment wrote that non-commissioned officers in his regiment removed their chevrons in late 1861 so that they would not stand out as targets. Moreover, those surviving original coats that do have chevrons often have them in black, rather than branch-of-service colour, suggesting that regulation-coloured stripes were not that commonly available.

Such chevrons as were worn appear to have been made by taking narrow strips of material and sewing them directly to the coat, rather than to a separate piece of material which was then sewn to the coat—the usual US Army practice.

coat' based on the civilian businessman's day coat and made with a lay-down collar and a single row of four or five buttons; of a length half-way between the frock and the 'roundabout', these coats had several outside slash pockets. These rather plain coats do not appear to have been made with either Austrian knots or branch-of-service coloured facings.

A double-breasted light grey blouse with a turn-over collar was also made regulation for fatigue dress. Such a garment does not actually seem to have been issued, however, at least in any quantity.

Because of the high cost of cloth and buttons, the typical Confederate soldier did not wear the regulation coat or blouse, except in fairly static posts. The study of photographs of Confederates in the field taken after 1862 shows that 71 per cent wear short-waisted, single-breasted 'roundabouts' with low standing collars. Union soldiers nick-named their Confederate opponents 'grey jackets' because of this typical dress. Frock coats, both single- and double-breasted, are worn by 18 per cent of the sample, while the remainder wear coats like officers' sack coats. Many of these sack coats were made by taking captured Union Army fatigue blouses, bleaching and re-dying them, and adding three buttons so that they had seven buttons down

the front. Sometimes a standing collar was added to replace the original falling style.

These 'roundabouts' became the standard dress from the very beginning; on 3 June 1861 the Acting Quartermaster General ordered 6,865 jackets to be issued, and from then on jackets were the norm—though this does not imply that they were uniform. The number of buttons down the front varied from five to ten; one school of thought holds that seven or nine buttons were most common on jackets issued in the Army of Northern Virginia, eight in the Army of the Tennessee, and six in the Trans-Mississippi Command—though this is difficult to verify.

In the study of photographs, 34 per cent of the men had epaulettes (i.e., cloth shoulder straps) on

North Carolina Private William A. Branch's brown homespun wool shell jacket is lined with dark brown polished cotton with an inside breast pocket on each side. The buttons, obscured here, are US Army general service pattern. (North Carolina Museum of History)

Four views of the all-grey uniform jacket worn by Private Joseph P. Lyle, 63rd Tennessee Infantry Regiment (despite the artillery buttons), Army of Northern Virginia. The jacket is medium grey, the lining white, and the buttons brass. Note how the buttons are attached by means of a string passing through the loops. (John D. Lyle)

This private wears a common variation of the shell jacket which has an epaulette on each shoulder. His shirt is white, probably the most common shirt colour. (Author's collection)

the whitish brown of ordinary dust'. A War Department clerk in Richmond reported seeing South Carolinians 'dressed in home-spun, dyed yellow from the bark of the butternut-tree'. And a captured Union soldier reported seeing the 1st Maryland Infantry, the only troops he saw after the Battle of Antietam 'that wore the regulation Confederate gray, all the other troops having assumed a sort of revised regulation of homespun butternut—a significant witness, we thought, to the efficacy of the blockade'. There is some reason to believe that by 1864 the Confederates had managed to organise a regular supply of dye, producing only grey uniforms from that point on. Jacket linings were usually cotton, in white, brown, or black 'polished' finish.

Mounted men were also authorised to receive a 'stable frock' during their enlistment. In the US Army this was a single-breasted garment made of plain white cotton drill or duck, to the same length as the sack coat, and worn when working in dirty stables or with horses. There is no evidence that these frocks were ever actually issued in the Confederate Army, however.

their jackets, while only six per cent displayed any branch-of-service coloured trim. Most jackets had slit-type pockets, sometimes closed with a bone button, inside the left breast, while some also had slash-type pockets on the outside. Some had loops of cloth about a $\frac{1}{2}$ in. wide on each side of the body, to keep the waist belt in place over the short-waisted jacket. These belt loops were sometimes sewn top and bottom, sometimes sewn at one end and buttoned at the other.

The largest variation was the colour. Greys ran from a very dark shade—most common in jackets issued in the Army of Northern Virginia—to a brownish grey. There is some indication, however, that brown was an even more common colour than grey, at least before 1864. This brown was produced by dying wool with a mixture of the oily nut of the white walnut (or 'butternut') tree, and copperas. The exact colours thus produced varied, one Union soldier reporting seeing dead after the Battle of South Mountain wearing uniforms of 'a color running all the way from a deep coffee brown up to

Other Uniform Items

Waistcoats

Waistcoats, called by Americans 'vests', were not part of regulation uniforms. They were, however, part of the typical contemporary American's wardrobe, and were therefore worn with his uniform, especially during the winter. Generally they were made of light-weight grey or brown wool or wool/cotton blend. Backs were generally of brown or black polished cotton, with a belt for size adjustment a couple of inches above and parallel to the bottom. Linings were usually white cotton. They usually had nine small buttons, often of civilian pattern, in a row down the front; and three or four slash pockets, two on the lower part and one or two on the chest. Most had standing collars—one original has a $1\frac{1}{2}$ in. tall collar—but many also had lay-down collars. Civilian waistcoats were also worn, although their use in the field appears to have been, at best, very limited.

Buttons

General Order Number Four called for brass buttons in two sizes, 1 in. and ⅞ in. in diameter, with the Roman letters 'A' for artillery, 'I' for infantry, 'C' for cavalry and 'R' for rifle officers. Enlisted artillerymen were to wear 'A' buttons, but men of other branches were to wear their regimental numbers. On 24 May 1861 it was ordered 'for the present let the buttons be made for infantry and a few for cavalry with I and C instead of numbers' for enlisted men; and no numbered buttons were apparently issued. Buttons, both Southern-made and imported, with these letters in Old English script were also widely issued.

In addition to these, some general service buttons bearing the Roman letters 'CSA' were also made and issued. Some of these have been found at Gettysburg, so they must have been in common use by mid-1863. Another general service button used a five-pointed star as a motif, one variety with the letters 'CS' within the star and another with the words 'SOUTHERN CONFEDERACY' around it. Buttons with a flag resting on crossed sabres, hilts down, also seem to have been issued to some cavalrymen. Captured US Army buttons, especially officers' buttons with a branch-of-service letter, were also widely used.

Although buttons were to have been brass, copper and pewter buttons bearing the regulation letters were also issued. Even the brass buttons were more copper than brass, often being simply stamped out with a copper wire shank attached to their backs. Imported brass buttons, on the other hand, were usually well made in three pieces. In fact, due to the South's poverty and lack of manufacturing industry, the most common buttons among enlisted men were probably those made of wood or bone. One veteran later recalled, 'Our buttons were made of wood, and soon parted company with our wretched garments.' The term 'brass buttons' was often used to mean an officer, which strongly suggests their rarity in the ranks.

Shirts

Confederate Army regulations called for the issue of three flannel shirts to each man every year. On 19 April 1861 these were described as white or red. Such appear to have been the most common colours. They were generally made pull-over

The top and front of this soldier's jacket collar are trimmed with a facing-colour tape, which also is used to edge the jacket front. The photograph was taken in Virginia. (Author's collection)

fashion, with one button at the collar and one at each cuff. Most had no pockets, although a few did have breast pockets. Eventually cotton became more popular than flannel: it was easier to wash, and vermin did not propagate as rapidly in cotton as in wool.

It appears that British Army shirts were also imported. One, worn by a 1st Virginia Artillery lieutenant, was made of blue and white striped cotton, with a 1 in.-wide neck band (instead of a collar) with one ⅞ in. bone button on it, and another of the same type half-way down the placket. The 1½ in.-wide cuffs each have one button. The shirt, now in the Museum of the Confederacy, is marked on the right front shirt tail in black ink with a British broad arrow and letters 'WD' over the markings EARLY & SMITH/C&M/1859. One cavalry sergeant wrote home in March 1865 that he had three linen collars to be worn with a detached collar shirt, which must have been of this kind. Separate collars must have been rare luxuries in the field, however.

Private Francis Jones, 8th Virginia Cavalry, wears a plain grey military-style waistcoat with a standing collar under his plain grey coat. The 8th served dismounted as infantry in West Virginia in early 1862. (Library of Congress)

Civilian shirts, brought from home, were also very popular. The Louisiana cavalry sergeant described, in a series of letters sent throughout the war, how he wore striped, blue linen, yellow checked, and bird's-eye calico shirts. Plaid and polka-dotted shirts also appear in original photographs of enlisted and commissioned Confederates.

Shirts were also worn as uniform jackets, especially early in the war. Generally these seem to have been made of wool flannel, buttoning all the way down the front, or at least to the waist. They have one or two slash pockets on the chest. Sleeves were quite full, with tight wristbands; and most of these shirts had collars. Most appear to have been made in plain colours, with tape of a contrasting colour (such as light blue or red) around the collar and pocket openings, and down the placket in front. Brass buttons, rather than wood or bone, also appear to have been common on these shirts.

A variation of this was the 'fireman's' or 'bib front' shirt, with a large chest plastron buttoned around the edges. These shirts were worn as uniform jackets by the Virginia Sussex Light Dragoons in 1861.

Another style worn as an outer garment, especially in the West, was the 'guerrilla shirt'. This was generally long-tailed, with two pockets on the chest and two lower down in which game and/or ammunition could be stored. It was made of heavy material, with a low scooped front ending just above the belt. This was edged in tape of contrasting colour, which was also used to decorate the pockets and sometimes the tails. The tails were sometimes worn outside the trousers, hunting shirt fashion. Beads or fancy needlework were often seen on the front. All colours, from scarlet to dull butternut, were used both for the basic material and for the trimmings.

Cravats

Confederate regulations called for black leather stocks to be issued, but this does not seem ever to have been done. Black or plaid civilian-type cravats were worn from time to time; but not, apparently, in the field, save perhaps by some officers. One Alabama soldier wrote home thanking his brother for clothing he had sent, 'except the cravat—if I was to put it on the boys would laugh at me'.

Vests

Vests, or 'undershirts' as Americans call them, were not issued but were sent from home. Louisiana cavalry Sgt. Edwin H. Fay wrote in September 1862 that he wanted 'an undershirt of Lowells if no net ones can be had'. In February 1863 his 'knitted one' was 'all coming to pieces'; and in November 1863 his 'net undershirt is a very handy thing and is much admired. I don't like the color though and the yarn is not twisted hard enough for service.'

Trousers

On 19 April 1861 the Confederate Army announced that it was going to issue 'steel gray pants' to its regular soldiers. On 25 May 1861 the New Orleans *Picayune* said regulation trousers were to be of 'sky-blue cloth, made full in the leg'. This turned out to agree with General Order Number Four, which added that regimental officers and non-commissioned officers were also to have a $1\frac{1}{4}$ in. branch-of-service colour stripe on each leg. Apparently relatively few such trousers were made by Confederate clothing plants, however, although some soldiers were able to obtain captured US Army sky-blue trousers. Waul's Texas Legion did receive an issue of 'good blue cloth pants' in November 1862.

Even so, when Sgt. Fay asked for some trousers from home he suggested that, for Southerners, 'blue is a bad color unless it is a very light blue. I shoot at blue clothes myself.' Indeed, Maj.Gen. Patrick Cleburne reported in October 1863 that a number of his men were killed by Confederate artillery: 'I can only account for this blunder from the fact that most of our men had on blue Federal pants.'

Instead, the most common trousers appear to have been made in the same colours as the jackets—grey and brown. And they were usually well worn. One veteran later recalled: 'It was a common sight to see all sorts of re-enforcements to the men's seats. On a pair of brown or butternut-colored trousers you would see a huge heart, square or star-shaped patch, according to the whim of the owner.' A 21st Virginia Infantry private later recalled that these patches were usually made of 'any material they could get. One man had the seat of his pants patched with bright red, and his knees patched with black. Another had used a piece of gray or brown blanket. There were, however, so few patches and so many holes that, when a Pennsylvania girl on the side of the road saw us pass and asked her mother how the officers were distinguished from the privates, the mother replied that it was easy enough: the officers' pants were patched, and the privates' pants were not.'

Typically, the trousers were made of wool, although the use of 'gray jeans' material was also widespread, especially in the West. A lieutenant from the 21st Alabama Infantry wrote to his wife in April 1862 that a brother officer had a pair of 'blanket pants and they do very well for every day service and really look well, though they are rough. . .' He, too, wanted a pair of trousers made from blanket material.

The usual pair of trousers had only two front pockets and sometimes a watch pocket, and either a belt or holes for laces over a vent at the back to adjust for size. There were no belt loops, and many had buttons of bone, wood or even metal for braces. Most had a small slit at the bottom of each leg seam. They were made without turn-ups.

Drawers

The one item the Confederate Army does appear to have supplied its men in abundance was white cotton drawers. Sgt. Fay wrote in September 1862 that he drew 'a pair of drawers (drilling) good stuff'. An original pair, worn by a lieutenant of the 1st Virginia Artillery, is made of white cotton, sewn with white thread. They have one-piece legs that would reach about two-thirds of the length of the wearer's leg, with slits on the seams inside and ties to fasten them around the leg. There is a 3 in. slit down the back with two eyelets for a fastening thong for

Issue Confederate buttons. *Top row*, infantry—Southern-made, as can be told from their relatively crude manufacture; *middle row*, artillery and cavalry; *bottom row*, riflemen and general service. The artilleryman's, rifleman's and general service buttons are British-made. (Author's collection)

Two members of the 6th Virginia Cavalry wear variations of the 'battle shirts' often seen in 1861. Note the US Army issue crossed sabres cap badge on the left-hand man's hat. Both men have Colt 0.36 in. calibre Navy revolvers. In the forefront of the cavalry action during the Second Manassas campaign, the 6th was reported as having been closer to Manassas Junction than any other Confederate cavalry outfit. (Library of Congress)

size adjustments. There is one bone button on the waistband and another half-way down the fly.

Issue drawers were noted for their poor fit. Fay reported one pair that 'would not fit any body in the world'; while a Mississippi soldier in the Army of the Tennessee wrote home: 'Dr Tankersley had a pair of Drawers that were too small and I had a pair that were too large. So we cut a piece out of mine and spliced his.'

Gaiters

Gaiters were not listed in regulations, nor were they apparently made for the Quartermaster Corps. They were, however, worn by a number of infantry units, especially early in the war. Lt.Gen. Richard Taylor described his brigade of the 6th, 7th, 8th and 9th Louisiana Infantry Regiments in early 1862 as wearing 'fresh clothing of gray with white gaiters'. White gaiters are also worn in a photograph of a colour sergeant of, it is believed, the 12th Virginia Infantry Regiment; the NCO holds an Army of Northern Virginia battleflag, which was not authorised until September 1861. The Hampton Legion Infantry received a full issue of 'leggings' on 30 September 1863, but it is unlikely that they were worn much after that.

The typical Southern gaiter appears to have been made of heavy white cotton duck with a leather strap passing under the boot. It reached to a point about half-way between the ankle and knee, and covered much of the top of the boot. It was fastened on the outside with either a row of bone or wood buttons, or by means of four or five small leather straps and buckles.

Some officers and mounted men wore painted black canvas or leather leggings. A painting of some Confederate infantrymen in Petersburg in late 1864 shows a company-grade officer wearing this type. Otherwise, few gaiters seem to have been worn that late in the war.

Boots

Boots, or 'shoes' as Americans called boots with laces, were described as 'ankle or Jefferson' for officers, and 'Jefferson' for enlisted men; they were both made in the South and imported from England. They were ankle-high, with two or three holes in front for leather laces. They were officially to be black, although reddish-brown ones were also made, and had square toes.

One veteran recalled that the English-made shoes were 'lined and filled with stiff paper, and after fording a few times they usually came to pieces'. Southern-made shoes weren't much better. The same veteran wrote: 'Generally made of green or at best half-cured leather, they soon took to roaming; after a week's wear the heel would be on the side, at an angle to the foot, and the vamp, in turn, would try to do duty as a sole. . . . They

Thomas I. Duvall, left, and William R. Duvall, both of the 3rd Missouri Infantry Regiment, wear versions of the 'battle' or 'guerrilla' shirt worn as outside wear. The 3rd, part of the 1st Missouri Brigade, were initially successful in the battle of Elkhorn Tavern, March 1862, capturing several artillery pieces and many supplies. The second day's fighting saw them overwhelmed and their colonel killed, forcing a retreat and a Union victory that gave the Federals control of northern Arkansas. (Dr Thomas Sweeney)

conformed to the weather, too. While hot and dry they would shrink like parchment, and when wet they just "slopped" all over your feet.'

In January 1864 Gen. Robert E. Lee wrote that he had received two pairs of sample shoes, one made in Richmond, Virginia, and the other in Columbus, Georgia. He didn't like the Richmond shoes because 'the face of the leather was turned out. That is, the side of the skin next the animal was turned out, which is contrary to the practice of the best makers.' The Columbus leather 'was not half tanned and the shoe was badly made. The soles of both [are] slight and would not stand a week's march in mud and water.'

He therefore obtained permission to have shoemakers in the Army of Northern Virginia make shoes for the troops. They were certainly needed, for there were almost always numbers of barefooted men in Confederate armies. Straggling during the

Army of Northern Virginia's march into Maryland—due in large part to soldiers going barefoot—caused Lee to have 13,000 less men than the 53,000 he should have had available for the Battle of Antietam. A 4th Texas private reported that in that Army many of the men were barefoot in late 1862; while a 1st Tennessee private recalled that in the winter of 1864–65 many of the soldiers of the Army of Tennessee 'were entirely barefooted'.

When there were shortages, improvisations were also made. The 4th Texas soldier recalled that in the winter of 1862 an order was issued calling for 'barefooted men to go to the slaughter pens, secure the hides that came off the beeves killed for the army, then make moccasins for their feet by taking the green hide, cutting a piece large enough to cover the feet, then turning the hairy side in. The order said to "wang the moccasins on with rawhide thongs", let them dry, and by that means secure a comfortable fit.' Another veteran recalled that some soldiers made similar moccasins over their issued shoes for winter wear, cutting them off again in the spring, and thereby preserving their shoes in good shape for the spring and summer campaigns.

Because of leather shortages, shoes with leather or canvas uppers and wooden soles were also issued. Both canvas shoes with leather soles and 'wood sole shoes' were listed in the clothing accounts of the 7th Louisiana Infantry Regiment of 1862–63. Captured US Army shoes and boots were very popular, when available, because of their high quality.

Cavalrymen and mounted officers preferred boots that reached to or slightly below the knee. These, too, were square toed and in either black or brown. Officially, mounted men were allowed to receive one pair of boots with two pairs of shoes, or 'bootees', instead of the four pairs of 'booties' issued to foot soldiers.

Col. Thomas Ruffin, 1st North Carolina Cavalry Regiment, wore these sky-blue trousers. They have 'mule ear' pocket flaps buttoned at each side. The lining material is white cotton. The 1st North Carolina were among the first Southern troops to detect the Federal advance during the Chancellorsville campaign, as some of their vedettes were captured while patrolling Kelley's Ford. (North Carolina Museum of History)

Socks

Each soldier was to receive four pairs of socks a year. This, even had the Army been able to issue them all, would not have been enough for the amount of marching it did. The result was that at least one US Army soldier reported finding a dead Confederate infantryman whose 'feet, wrapped in rags, had coarse shoes upon them, so worn and full of holes that they were only held together by means of pieces of thick twine'. Knitted socks sent from home were common, as were captured US Army socks. They were usually white, and made from cotton and/or wool. They were often worn with the ends of the trouser legs tucked into them; since they were made without elastic at the tops, when they were worn as gaiters they were usually tied in place with string.

Overcoats

According to General Order Number Four, overcoats were to be of cadet grey cloth with a stand-up collar, double-breasted, with a cape. Foot soldiers were to have a cape reaching the elbows; mounted men, capes reaching the cuff.

In fact, however, overcoats were rarely issued. A soldier in Stanford's Mississippi Battery noted in his diary of 29 October 1862 that he 'was lucky enough to draw an overcoat this evening—well, boys, I am willing to divide [the use of] it these cold nights when on duty'. The rareness of issue was not because of any unwillingness on the part of the Army: indeed, in October 1863 the Quartermaster General said that overcoat material was one of the three things he needed most.

Some of this material was obtained from England. A New Jersey chaplain saw prisoners in the fall of 1863, 'some wearing overcoats of English frieze, whose materials had run the blockade, and others in the common, homespun Negro cloth, dyed with the juice of the butternut or other vegetable tincture'. The blue English material was of a 'much darker hue' than the sky-blue US Army overcoats, another Union soldier later wrote.

A Southern-made overcoat worn by Col. Ellison Capers, 24th South Carolina Infantry, and now in the Confederate Museum, is tan in colour, with four large state buttons in a single row down the front and seven small ones on the cape, which reaches to just below the elbows. The collar could be worn standing or lying down. Another Southern-made

overcoat was painted by a veteran as being dark grey with a black stripe about an inch wide some 6 ins. from its bottom edge. It has long, rolled-up cuffs, and a cape worn around the head for warmth. Other contemporary paintings also show grey overcoats being worn.

A Richmond Howitzers private later recalled that most soldiers discarded their issued overcoats, since they could capture 'one about the time it would be needed. Nearly every overcoat in the army in the later years of the war was one of Uncle Sam's captured from his boys,' he wrote. At times these were dyed to change the sky-blue colour. The captured overcoats of the 104th Illinois, for example, were dyed black and issued to Morgan's Raiders for their 1862 Kentucky raid. For the most part, however, the soldiers seem to have left them in their original colour. The sergeant major of the 1st

Col. Thomas Ruffin's overcoat. Note the folded-up cuffs, and the collar tab to fasten the collar together in cold weather. The detachable cape is missing. (North Carolina Museum of History)

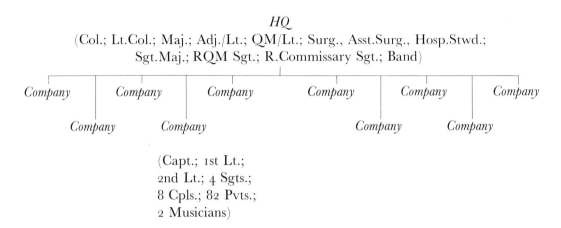

CONFEDERATE INFANTRY REGIMENT

HQ
(Col.; Lt.Col.; Maj.; Adj./Lt.; QM/Lt.; Surg., Asst.Surg., Hosp.Stwd.;
Sgt.Maj.; RQM Sgt.; R.Commissary Sgt.; Band)

Company   *Company*   *Company*   *Company*   *Company*   *Company*

Company   *Company*   *Company*   *Company*

(Capt.; 1st Lt.;
2nd Lt.; 4 Sgts.;
8 Cpls.; 82 Pvts.;
2 Musicians)

The regulation strength of just over 1,000 all ranks was almost unknown in practice: on campaign the average regimental strength was somewhere between 400 and 700. Apart from sickness and casualties, chronic desertion also weakened both Union and Confederate armies. Even patriotic volunteers completely lacked the regular soldier's attitude to service. They were more likely to desert between battles than during them, feeling that they had 'done their bit' and that any sensible man could now feel entitled to return to care for his family and farm. Conscription, introduced in April 1862, replaced the earlier, unsatisfactory system of twelve-month voluntary enlistments with forced service for the duration of the war for any enlistee between the ages of 18 and 35. It was much resented, and did little to lessen desertion. It should be noted, however, that the Confederate soldier generally displayed great loyalty, endurance and determination on campaign: it is a mistake to see the desertion rate through 20th-century eyes, since it sprang from attitudes foreign to the modern student of military life.

Regiments were almost invariably brigaded with other units from the same state, and the brigade—named after its commander—was the focus of *esprit de corps*. The Confederate Army was also notably more successful than the US Army in maintaining the strength and cohesion of the regiment. Regiments were kept in being, even when severely weakened, by drafts of replacements; this ensured the growth of a regimental tradition, and an effective mix of veterans and recruits in any one unit at any given time.

The numbers of regiments in each brigade, and of brigades in each division, varied considerably according to unit strength. *Longstreet's Corps* in April 1865 provides a typical enough example of the late war period:

Pickett's Division:
Steuart's Bde.: 9th, 14th, 38th, 53rd, 57th Virginia
Corse's Bde.: 15th, 17th, 29th, 30th, 32nd Virginia
Hunton's Bde.: 8th, 18th, 19th, 28th, 56th Virginia
Terry's Bde.: 1st, 3rd, 7th, 11th, 24th Virginia
Field's Division:
Perry's Bde.: 4th, 15th, 44th, 47th, 48th Alabama
Anderson's Bde.: 7th, 8th, 9th, 11th, 59th Georgia
Benning's Bde.: 2nd, 15th, 17th, 20th Georgia
Bratton's Bde.: 1st, 5th, 6th South Carolina, 2nd SC Rifles,

Palmetto Sharpshooters (SC)
Gregg's Bde.: 3rd Arkansas, 1st, 4th, 5th Texas
Kershaw's Division:
Du Bose's Bde.: 16th, 18th, 24th Georgia, 3rd Bn. GA
Sharpshooters, Cobb's and Phillips's GA Legions
Humphrey's Bde.: 13th, 17th, 18th, 21st Mississippi
Simms's Bde.: 10th, 50th, 51st, 53rd Georgia
Artillery:
Haskell's Bn. (four batteries)
Huger's Bn. (six batteries)

South Carolina Infantry Regiment was trapped by a sudden attack in March 1865. 'Wearing a blue overcoat', a regimental member later recalled, 'he has been mistaken by the enemy in the dim light for one of their own men, even talking with him.'

Capes were sometimes worn by themselves in place of full-length overcoats.

Sashes

Infantry and artillery officers were to wear red silk net sashes with silk bullion fringe ends, the ends to hang no more than 18 ins. below the waist when the sash was worn beneath the sword belt. The actual shade varied from scarlet through crimson to magenta. Cavalry officers were to wear the same type of sash in yellow silk. Sergeants were to wear similar sashes in red and yellow worsted respectively. At least one colour sergeant, of what is believed to be a Virginia infantry regiment, was photographed some time after September 1861 wearing such a sash round his waist under his belt; but it seems that sashes were rare in the field.

Field Signs

In early 1861, when men of both sides wore blue and grey fairly indiscriminately, various field signs were used. At the battle of First Manassas the Washington Artillery, who were uniformed in blue, wore red flannel bands round their left arms. Some other blue-clad Confederates appear to have done the same; but a plan to extend this sign to the entire army was dropped when it was discovered that the Northern forces were doing the same thing.

White hat bands were worn by soldiers under Maj.Gen. John Magruder in mid-1861, while his scouts had white sashes worn 'from shoulder to hip'. White hat badges, 'about an inch wide and six long', were also worn by soldiers under Generals Loring and Jackson in the Valley of Virginia as late as December 1861, and possibly even early in 1862.

Zouave and Chasseur Uniforms

In 1860 a fad for wearing copies of French Zouave and Chasseur dress swept the North. This had some influence in the South too; and a number of so-called Zouave units were formed in the states from Texas to Virginia. Because of difficulties in obtaining even anything like regulation uniforms, let alone copies of the elaborate and ornate Zouave dress, few of these uniforms lasted more than a few months unless kept packed away in trunks. A private in the 63rd Pennsylvania Infantry wrote home on 26 June 1862 that his unit had recently been 'opposed by the Fourth Georgians. The Georgians were dressed in a fancy French zouave uniform, which caused our men to hesitate'—so some Zouave uniforms must have lasted at least that late.

The most famous such unit were the Louisiana Zouaves, who wore short blue jackets (which appear to have been replaced with brown in late 1861) trimmed with red; red shirts; red fezzes; blue and white striped trousers; and white gaiters. A uniform thought to have been worn by an officer of the Richmond Zouaves (Co. E, 44th Virginia Infantry Regiment) has a dark blue jacket fastened by a tab at the throat and edged in gold. Each cuff is decorated with a white 'clover leaf' edged in gold. There are five Virginia State buttons on each cuff and two large ones at the neck. The trousers are baggy, made of scarlet wool with a gold stripe down each leg. The uniform also includes a blue wool sash with scarlet fringe, and a scarlet French-style képi trimmed in gold according to Army regulations.

To keep up the complete Zouave illusion, Southern units, like the French regiments they copied, appear to have recruited *vivandières*—female sutlers—who accompanied the units. These women usually wore short wool jackets of the same colour and trim as those worn by the men; wide-brimmed, plumed hats; and trousers which were woollen from a point just above where they would appear under the skirt, and cotton above that. They were sometimes armed with revolvers; and often carried wooden casks filled with water, or stronger stuff, for the men. A Southern society lady in Richmond noted in her diary on 13 July 1861: 'Today in the drawing room I saw a *vivandière*, in the flesh. She was in the uniform of her regiment, but wore Turkish pantaloons. She frisked about in her hat and feathers, did not uncover her head as a man would have done, played the piano, sang war songs. She had no drum but she gave us a rataplan!'

Confederate cannoneers haul a 12-pdr. bronze 'Napoleon' gun up a steep hill. Note that many of them are wearing only their shirts in action. (*Battles & Leaders of the Civil War*)

Accoutrements

Beltplates

The 1863 Confederate Ordnance Manual called for the foot soldier's beltplate to be 'brass, oval, 3.5 inches long by 2.25 inches wide, stamped with the letters "CS", two studs and one hook, brass.' A similar plate was to be placed on the cartridge box flap, although these are quite rare and apparently were not produced after 1862. From camp sites where the beltplates have been recovered it appears that such plates first appeared in early 1862. The study of photographed enlisted men indicates that nine per cent of them wore this style of plate. Variations include a cast brass plate with 11 stars around the edge, which was apparently worn by a Western brigade; and a stamped brass, lead-backed plate bearing the letters 'CSA', which was found at the site of the Battle of Antietam.

This plate was a copy of the US Army infantry beltplate and, in fact, the US plate was more common than the CS one, with 18 per cent of photographed soldiers wearing the US issue. Finds also indicate that sometimes the front of the US plates were removed and the hooks worn by themselves.

The study of photographs also revealed that six per cent of enlisted men wore rectangular cast brass plates marked 'CSA'. This type may have been designed in response to 1861 regulations which called for a gilt rectangular sword belt plate, 'two inches wide, with a raised bright rim; a silver wreath of laurel encircling the "arms of the Confederate States"'. No beltplates exactly fitting this description have ever been found. The plainer 'CSA' rectangular plates appear to have been made first in the Atlanta Arsenal, and their widest distribution was among troops of the Army of Tennessee. It appears that troops of the Stonewall Brigade, among other Army of Northern Virginia soldiers, were also issued this type of plate. Francis Minchemer, of Griffin, Georgia, was contracted to produce 4,000 of them, using scrap brass from the Atlanta Arsenal. They were about $2\frac{3}{4}$ ins. by 2 ins.; and, as with all Southern-made brass objects, the heavy concentration of copper in the alloy gave the metal a strong red shade. These plates seem to have been issued for the first time in 1862.

Some Western Confederates also wore cast brass rectangular beltplates made with slightly curved edges and bearing the letters 'CS'.

The most common Confederate soldier's waist belt buckle was a plain frame type, usually brass. Fully 50 per cent of the plates seen in photographs are of this type—a percentage confirmed by excavations at camp and battle sites. They appeared in several styles. One was the 'Georgia' buckle, which had two prongs cast as part of the

The most common types of Confederate issue beltplates. The two-piece mounted man's buckle (*top*) is somewhat unusual in that most examples are made with the belt loops standing further away from the wreath than is seen in this example. The *bottom* example is of stamped copper with a lead backing and iron belt hooks, while the other two are cast brass with a very reddish, copper tint to them. (Author's collection)

1: Private, Infantry, 1861
2: Private, 4th Texas Inf.Regt., 1861
3: 1st Sgt., Louisiana Infantry, 1861

A

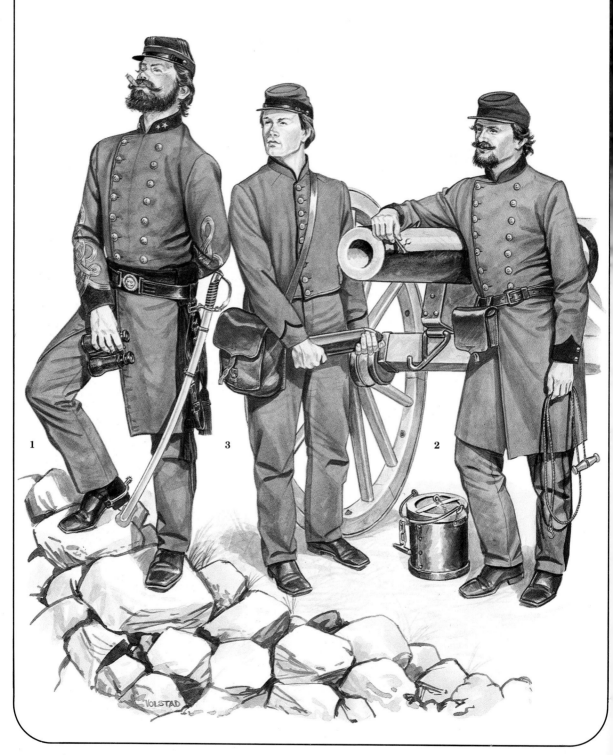

B

1: Captain, Cavalry, 1862
2: 1st Lt., Alabama Cavalry, 1862
3: Sgt.Maj., Cavalry, 1862

C

1: Private, 2nd Maryland Inf.Regt., 1863
2: Bandsman, 1863
3: Cpl., President's Guard, 1863

D

1: Private, Infantry, 1863
2: Ord.Sgt., 28th NC Inf.Regt., 1863
3: Drummer, Infantry, 1863

E

1: Major, Artillery, 1864
2: QM Sgt., Artillery, 1864
3: 2nd Lt., Artillery, 1864

F

1: Private, Infantry, 1864
2: Sgt., 4th Kentucky Inf. Regt., 1864
3: 1st Lt., 2nd Regt. SC Rifles, 1864

G

1: Private, Infantry, 1865
2: Col., 44th Georgia Inf. Regt., 1865
3: Private, Infantry, 1865

VOLSTAD

frame; some of these were marked 'McElroy & Hunt, Macon, Georgia'. Another had a separate prong of forked shape, with a single prong dividing into two spikes; this type was usually 4 ins. by 2⅔ ins., although sometimes slightly smaller. A third common type had two separate prongs attached to the centre post. It would appear that the frame buckle was more common in the Army of Northern Virginia, while Western Confederates made more use of beltplates.

Quite a number of plain cast brass and sheet iron beltplates, both oval and rectangular, have been found at camp sites throughout the Southern states. These came in a wide variety of sizes.

The typical Confederate mounted and officer's beltplate was a two-piece copy of the M1841 US foot artillery plate. The 'spoon', or 'male' part, bearing the letters 'CS', fitted into a circular 'female' piece bearing a laurel wreath. Most of these plates have been found in the Virginia area. Some rectangular sword belt plates bearing the Roman letters 'CS' are also known, but these were quite rare. British-made 'snake' buckles were also common. British-made rectangular cast brass beltplates, bearing the Army of Northern Virginia battleflag within a wreath, were also issued; it has been suggested that these were made from a basic design used by British yacht owners.

Belts

Infantry belts were plain black or brown leather. Known alternatives adopted because of leather shortages included heavy cotton cloth, sometimes in several layers stitched together and painted black; and natural white webbing.

Sword belts had 'keeps', or half the two-piece beltplate permanently attached to one end and an adjustable part on the other. A hook and two slings for the sabre were attached to the left of the belt, the rear sling being worn at about the centre of the back and dropping longer than the front sling. Some had 'Sam Browne'-type shoulder belts passing from the left rear, over the right shoulder and down to hook on at the left front; these were, however, uncommon.

Cap Boxes

The typical Southern-made cap box was of brown or black leather, the pouch 2½ ins. deep and 1¼ ins. thick. It had a lambswool lining, and an inner flap separate from the outer flap which covered the entire front. Iron nipple picks were often inserted into a loop inside the pouch on the right. The most common flap shape was a 'shield' with a separate

Two russet brown Southern-made cap boxes. The one on the left has the typical Southern single belt loop and a pewter stud. (Author's collection)

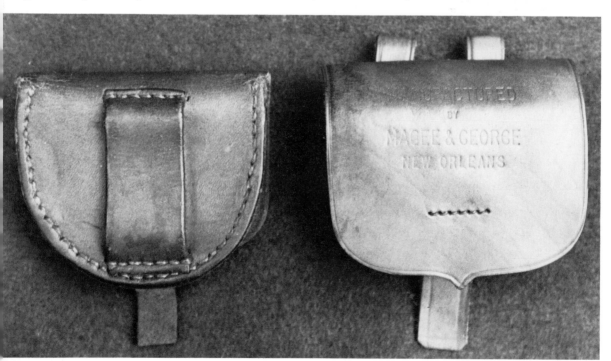

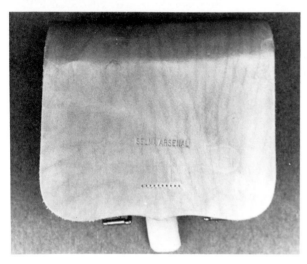

The back and front of a Southern-made russet brown cartridge box; it could be carried either on a shoulder belt or a waist belt. (Author's collection)

buttoned on to a brass stud. A second piece of leather passed from side to side to form the front under the flap. There was an inner flap, lambswool lining, and a single belt loop. The dimensions were $2\frac{5}{8}$ ins. by $\frac{3}{4}$ in. by 2 inches.

Issue British Army cap pouches were also imported, and US Army cap boxes were used when captured. One veteran artilleryman reported that many soldiers threw away their cap boxes and carried caps in their pockets. Another veteran infantryman also recalled carrying his caps in a waistcoat pocket.

Bayonets and Scabbards

'The infantry found out that bayonets were not of much use, and did not hesitate to throw them, with the scabbard, away,' recalled a Richmond Howitzers veteran. This appears to have been generally true—although, after one hand-to-hand combat, men of the 4th Texas Infantry who had previously discarded their bayonets made every effort to replace them.

The Southern-made rifled musket bayonet was a triangular-section socket type with an 18 in. blade and a 3 in. socket, made of iron with a steel tip. It was carried in a brown or black leather scabbard, often with an iron or tin chape, with the frog sewn to the scabbard. The imported Enfield bayonet was similar, but the black leather scabbard had a 3 in.-long brass chape and $1\frac{1}{4}$ in.-long throat. It was slipped into a black leather frog, a hook on the face of the brass throat engaging with a slit in the frog.

Rifles took sabre bayonets. Typically, these had 22 in. blades and 5 in. cast brass handles. Scabbards were of black leather with brass chapes and throats and buckled into separate frogs. Because the sabre bayonet required so much material—and was not much used, in any case—its production was ordered to be abandoned from 14 January 1864.

Cartridge Boxes

Southern-made cartridge boxes were copies of US Army patterns. One basic type was a copy of the box made for the M1842 percussion musket. It was made to be carried on a shoulder belt. Inside it had two tin containers, each holding 20 cartridges; a separate implement pouch was placed on the front surface of the box, underneath the outer and inner flaps.

central fastening strap. Fastening studs, mounted to engage slits in these straps, were of brass, lead, or even wood. The box had a single belt loop on the back, just over an inch wide, or two narrow ones instead. Many were marked on the front flap with the maker's name, e.g., 'C.S. ARSENAL/BATON ROUGE, LA,'; or, more rarely, with the letters 'CS'.

A major variation of the cap box originated in England, although some of this type were also made in the South. One piece of leather, edged with two tooled rows, ran from the bottom, up to form the back, and over to become the cover, which

CONFEDERATE CAVALRY REGIMENT

```
                              HQ
          (Col.; Lt.Col.; Maj.; Adj./Lt.; Sgt.Maj.; QM Sgt.)
```

| Company (or 'Squadron') | Company | Company | Company | Company | Company |

| Company | Company (Capt.; 1st Lt.; 2 × 2nd Lt.; 5 Sgts.; 4 Cpls.; Farrier; Smith; 60 to 80 Privates) | | Company | Company |

It is well known that in 1861–63 Confederate cavalry outclassed their Union opponents. Recruited among a rural population accustomed to riding from childhood, and led by a horse-conscious country 'squirearchy', the Southern regiments were also handled better in being concentrated from the first into a corps and committed in strength, at a time when Union units were weakened by dispersion. (Union reforms from 1863 on, coupled with the Union's much greater resources, reversed this situation in the second half of the war.)

Regiments were gathered into brigades—anything from two to six regiments, depending upon strength; and brigades—again, up to six of them—into divisions. In April 1865 the Cavalry Corps of the Army of Northern Virginia had four divisions totalling ten brigades, plus two artillery battalions totalling five batteries. *Fitzhugh Lee's Division* may be taken as representative:

Munford's Bde.: 1st, 2nd, 3rd, 4th Virginia
Payne's Bde.: 5th, 6th, 8th Virginia, 36th VA Bn.
Gary's Bde.: 7th Georgia, 7th South Carolina, Hampton's Legion (SC), 24th Virginia

It is interesting that Confederate cavalry, for all their reputation among their enemies, enjoyed no vast popularity among their unmounted compatriots. Like infantry the world over, the foot soldiers were inclined toward contempt for the often invisible cavalry; Gen. D. H. Hill is said to have offered a reward to anyone who could find him a dead cavalryman, killed in action 'with his spurs on'. The Confederate troopers, under leaders such as Stuart and Morgan, excelled at long-range raids and scouts, cutting up Union lines of communication and supply. They were less impressive when working in closer harness with the rest of the army, and 'Jeb' Stuart's failure to keep Gen. Lee informed of Union movements at Gettysburg is notorious.

The dismissive remarks of foreign observers like Col. Fremantle, who judged Confederate cavalry harshly by the standards of Horse Guards, must be understood in context. The firepower of infantry rifled muskets made any kind of classic charge against infantry formed up on the battlefield a suicidal affair, and Civil War cavalry avoided such foolishness. They skirmished vigorously with pistols, carbines, shotguns and sabres; they often fought on foot, though hampered by their lack of modern carbines; and they were both versatile and enduring. Their main handicap lay in the difficulty of mounting them. Confederate troopers had to provide their own horses. If the horse was killed, and the rider was unable to find himself another, then he became an infantryman. This was no way to keep up the strength of the cavalry—and no way to encourage audacity in battle.

A second basic type was a copy of the percussion rifle box introduced in 1850. This was made to be carried on a waist belt; it had a single large tin container for all 40 cartridges, and both outer and inner flaps, but lacked the separate implement pouch.

The final type was a copy of the US 1855 model. This was made for either a waist or shoulder belt, with two tin containers and an implement pouch. All three boxes had brass fastening studs, although, because of shortages, Southern makers also used tin, wood and lead as well. Many Southern-made boxes used components of all three models, e.g., a single tin inside, but also an implement pouch; many also appeared in brown as well as regulation black leather. The US boxes had oval brass box plates, like waist belt plates; these were extremely rare on Southern-made boxes, although a few Confederate examples have the outer flap impressed with the letters 'CS'. A very large number of British Army cartridge boxes were also imported.

Shoulder belts were generally of black or brown leather, although numbers were also made from several layers of cotton cloth stitched together and painted black. No cartridge box shoulder strap beltplates were issued by the Confederate Army.

Holsters

Confederate-made holsters were copied from US Army patterns. They completely covered the pistol, with a flap that fastened down on the front of the holster. Supply shortages inevitably caused minor variations. Few holsters had the small piece of leather used to stop the end, or bottom, which was found on the US models. Instead of buttoning to brass studs, many flaps were shut by slipping a strap into a slot made by sewing another strap across the front of the holster. Brown, rather than black, leather was commonly used. The major difference, however, was that many of these holsters were so made that the pistol butt pointed to the wearer's rear, instead of to the front, as in US holsters.

Haversacks

The haversack was one thing that the Confederacy could provide easily, and it seems to have done so in abundance. In fact, one recruit recalled being issued no accoutrements other than two haversacks, 'miserably weak and sleazy, made of thin cotton cloth,' upon his enlistment in 1863. White cotton cloth haversacks were regulation, and were to be marked in black on the flap with the regimental number and name, the company letter, and the soldier's number. This appears to have been done only rarely.

The typical haversack was made of white cotton or drilling about 11 ins. square. It had a pointed flap fastened with a single tin, pewter, wood or bone button. The buttonhole and the button attachment point were often reinforced with additional material. A second bag, of the same size as the outer bag, was sometimes buttoned inside the haversack in order to keep food separate from other contents.

The relatively waterproof US Army issue haversack was greatly preferred; indeed, according to a veteran of the 1st South Carolina Infantry Regiment, it was rare to see Southern-made haversacks in the Army of Northern Virginia after the spring of 1862.

Water-bottles

The most common Southern-made water-bottle (or 'canteen', as Americans called it) was of tin, made drum-style, with flat faces, a single strip forming the sides, three loops to take a leather or cotton sling, and a round spout with a wood or cork stopper.

They were some 5 to 7 ins. in diameter and $\frac{1}{2}$ to $2\frac{1}{2}$ ins. thick. Leather slings usually had a buckle for size adjustment. Canteens similar to this, but made of cedar or sometimes cherry, with three iron sling loops and spouts of either tin or turned wood, were also issued; and numbers of British Army wooden canteens were imported. Southern firms also produced some tin copies of the round, wool-covered US Army canteen, made of two shallow-domed 'dishes' welded edge to edge; Confederate examples differed from the US model in that the spout was tin rather than pewter.

As with the haversack, veterans agreed that the US Army canteen was the most favoured type among Confederates. One of them wrote that 'in the middle of the war and later, to see equipment of Southern make was somewhat of a curiosity'. Another said that it was the mark of a new recruit to carry a Confederate canteen, since picking up a US one on any battlefield was an easy task. Be that as it may, the most common Confederate artefact found on camp and battle sites is the lowly tin 'drum' canteen.

Knapsacks

According to regulations, Confederate troops were to be issued black-painted knapsacks, which were to be marked with $1\frac{1}{2}$ in. regimental numbers—in white for the infantry and in yellow for the artillery.

A Southern-made tin 'drum'-style canteen. These are the single most common Southern-made items found today at battle and camp sites. (Author's collection)

The company letter and soldier's number were to be marked inside the knapsack. In spite of these detailed specifications, however, knapsacks were rarely issued in practice. The photographic study of enlisted men indicates that 18 per cent wore knapsacks, while the rest wore blanket rolls, mostly from the left shoulder to the right hip.

Such knapsacks as there were came in three main categories: captured US Army ones, mostly still marked with the original owner's regimental designations; imported British-made copies of British Army models; and Southern-made types. The latter were usually limp, black-painted canvas bags some 15 ins. by 16 ins. by 3 ins. when fully packed. The shoulder straps, about 1 in. wide, passed through loops on the top surface and continued across the rear or visible face of the bag, forming an 'X'-shape, and fastening with buckles and/or hooks under the bottom surface. There was no provision for a blanket to be attached to the outside of the bag.

Blankets

Blankets, too, came in three kinds: captured US Army blankets, civilian blankets from home, and Army-issued blankets. One of the latter, in a private collection, is light brown, about 5 ft. square, with a 5 in.-wide dark brown stripe around its sides. The wool is homespun with a herringbone weave.

Shelter-halves and Waterproofs

US Army issue waterproofs ('gum blankets') were of cotton coated with black rubber, like oilcloth. The South was not able to manufacture such items, so whenever possible Confederates tried to obtain captured ones. According to Lt.Col. J. W. Mallet, Superintendent of Confederate Ordnance Laboratories, 'extensive use was made of heavy cotton cloth, for some purposes in double or quadruple thicknesses heavily stitched together, treated with one or more coats of drying oil. Sheets of such cloth were issued to the men . . . for sleeping on damp ground. . . . Linseed oil answered best for making this cloth, and much was imported through the blockade, but it was eked out to some extent by fish oil. . . .'

Shelter-halves, two of which buttoned together to form a two-man tent, were not made by the Confederates, although many soldiers did manage to obtain US Army models. Tents were, however, generally discouraged. On 6 February 1864 the Army of Tennessee ordered that each corps headquarters was allowed only three tents; each brigade and regimental headquarters, two; and 'as many flies for the sick of the regiments as corps commanders may designate'. Only one wagon per division was allowed to carry tents.

Waterproofs and captured shelter-halves were wrapped around the blanket rolls when carried by the individual soldier.

Weapons

Infantry Longarms

It was not until late 1862 that the Confederates were able to replace obsolete flintlock muskets with percussion muskets—many of these still being smoothbore—among its frontline troops. This was accomplished with weapons from three sources: the US Army, foreign countries, and local makers.

The US Army, mostly armed with M1861 Springfield rifled muskets and P1853 Enfields, was possibly the major supplier. The Confederate Ordnance Department reported on 30 September 1864 that 45,000 small arms had been captured, compared to only 30,000 imported and 20,000 produced in the South during that year. The Ordnance Department also reported that after the Battle of Chancellorsville in May 1863 they recovered 26,000 rifles and rifled muskets from the

Lockplate of the first type of Richmond Armory rifled musket. The later model had a lower 'hump' to the lockplate and was stamped 'CS' over the 'RICHMOND, VA.' (**Russ Pritchard**)

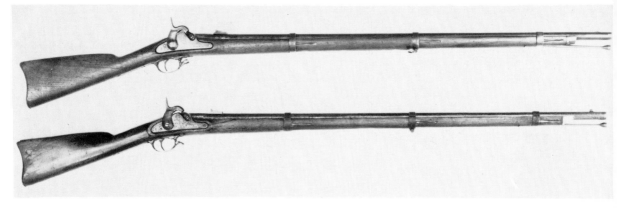

Richmond Armory rifled muskets, the earliest type on top and the later model below it. (Russ Pritchard/Milwaukee Public Museum)

field: of these, 10,000 were thought to have been discarded by Confederate soldiers who traded them for better weapons found on the field.

Imports played a large role in arming the infantry. Of these, 75 per cent were English made, mostly copies of the P1853 Enfield; 20 per cent were from Austria, mostly the M1854 rifled musket, of which 100,000 were imported; and the remaining five per cent were from France, Belgium and various German states. The major English supplier was the London Armoury which, by February 1863, had shipped 70,980 rifled muskets, 9,715 rifles and 354 carbines to Southern ports. Thereafter this company shipped 1,300 rifled muskets a month until the end of the war.

Captured rifle- and musket-making machinery from the Harper's Ferry Armory was also sent South. Machinery for making rifled muskets went to the Richmond Armory, which produced some 11,762 weapons. These rifled muskets were close copies of the US Springfield, except that the lockplate had the 'hump' designed for a Maynard primer, and brass nose caps and butt plates were used. Rifle machinery went to Fayetteville, North Carolina, where some 20,000 rifles were produced before that city's capture in 1865. The rifles were copies of the US M1855, 49½ ins. long. They had locks like those of the Springfield, and brass barrel bands, nose caps, butt plates and trigger guards.

Copies of the Enfield rifle were produced by Cook & Brother, a private concern which manufactured some 20,000 'two-band' rifles and a much smaller number of 'three-band' rifled muskets. Poor copies of the Enfield were also

produced in the Tyler, Texas, Armory. Other Southern private makers copied the M1842 rifle, albeit in relatively small numbers.

A handful of British-made sharpshooters' rifles were also imported. These were of the Enfield type, which resembled the P1858 short rifle; the Whitworth rifle; and the Kerr, which was similar to the P1858 Enfield. All of these models were 0.45 in. calibre.

Each longarm was fitted to take a sling, yet not all weapons were actually issued with slings: indeed, the Richmond Arsenal issued only 115,087 musket and carbine slings in three and a half years, although it issued 323,231 longarms. Until 1864 the average issue sling was made of cotton cloth, with a leather-reinforced section punched to take the adjustment hook. After 1864 leather slings were issued.

Cavalry Longarms

In March 1862 an ordnance officer wrote that Col. Nathan Bedford Forrest had said 'that the double-barrel shotgun is the best gun with which the cavalry can be armed'. However, a more traditional weapon in the shape of a single-shot, muzzle-loading copy of the Enfield carbine was adopted as the regulation Confederate cavalry longarm in October 1863. A factory was set up to make these at Tallassee, Alabama; but it was not until April 1865 that their first 900 carbines were shipped—too late to be of much use. Such carbines were also made by Cook & Brother, and imported from England; and the Richmond Armory made some 2,800 short carbine versions of their rifled muskets. A number of Southern makers also produced copies of the muzzle-loading, single-shot M1854 US carbine.

Breech-loading carbines, as used by most US

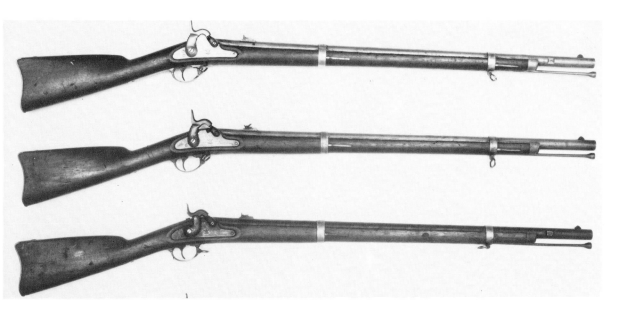

The three models of Fayetteville Armory rifles, the earliest at the top and latest at the bottom. Like the Richmond weapons, these were made with dies captured from the Harper's Ferry Arsenal. (Russ Pritchard/Milwaukee Public Museum)

Detail of the lockplate of the final Fayetteville rifle, showing the distinctive S-shaped hammer. These were among the finest Southern weapons made. (Russ Pritchard)

cavalry regiments, were more efficient and faster shooting, and were therefore prized as war booty. The S.C. Robinson Arms Manufactory was set up in Richmond to make copies of the breech-loading Sharps carbine in 1862. The factory produced some 1,882 of them before it was taken over by the government on 1 March 1863; eventually its production totalled 5,200 carbines. The 'Richmond Sharps' quickly got a bad reputation for bursting on firing, however. Even though the rumour was unfounded, it persisted, and the 'Richmond Sharps' remained unpopular with the cavalry throughout the war.

Other breech-loading carbines were made by George Morse (about 1,000 weapons, using brass centrefire cartridges), and J. H. Tarpley (this type having a rising breech to take a paper-wrapped cartridge). Other breech-loaders which used a paper-wrapped cartridge were the 'Perry' or 'Maynard' carbine; and the 'rising block' carbines, whose manufacturers are unknown today.

Weapons which took a brass cartridge, such as the Morse carbine and captured Northern models like the Burnside and Spencer, presented the Confederate Ordnance Department with a prob-

lem. They had virtually no facilities to make such ammunition; it was not until far on in the war that they finally set up suitable plants, and by then it was too late to do them much good. This meant that many of the best captured US Army carbines could not be used by the Confederates, except on an individual basis with chance-found pouchfuls of cartridges.

Handguns

According to the Confederate Ordnance Department's *Field Manual* of 1862, 'Colt's pistol is used in our service, and is constructed on the revolving principle, with a cylinder containing six chambers and a rifled barrel.' Copies of these revolvers, usually in 0.36 in. calibre, were made by Griswold & Gunnison (production: 3,600 revolvers), Leech & Rigdon (350), Rigdon & Ansley (2,330), The Columbus Fire Arms Manufacturing Co. (7,500),

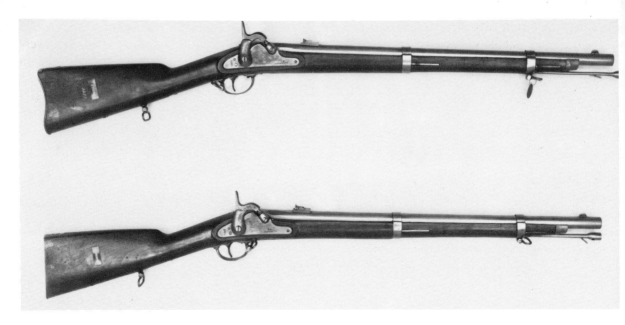

Two muzzle-loading Richmond Armory cavalry carbines. They are little more than cut-down infantry rifled muskets. (Russ Pritchard/Milwaukee Public Museum)

and Schneider & Glassick (14). Some of these, notably the Griswold & Gunnison models, used brass frames rather than steel because of supply shortages.

Spiller & Burr and the Macon Arsenal produced some 1,400 brass-framed copies of the Northern Whitney 0.36 in. calibre revolver. Quantities of imported Deane-Adams, Beaumont-Adams, Kerr Army and William Tranter revolvers came from England; and Lefaucheu pinfire, Devisem, Raphael, Perrin, and Houllier et Blanchard revolvers came from France.

Edged Weapons

Except for special swords for musicians, which were not made in the South, the Confederates copied every regulation US model sword. Officially, these were copies of the US M1840 cavalry sabre, the M1860 light cavalry sabre, the M1833 dragoon sabre, the M1840 light artillery sabre, the M1833 foot artillery sword, the M1840 non-commissioned officer's sword, and the M1850 foot officer's sword.

Generally, Southern-made swords are marked by their crudeness. Blades rarely had the stopped double fullers of Northern swords. Grips were usually wrapped in oilcloth or brown leather secured by a single, or at best double, strand of copper, brass or iron wire, often untwisted. Hilts

were crudely cast, or even beaten out of sheet brass; heavy copper concentrations gave them a red appearance. Metal scabbards often had brass rings, chapes and throats, while leather scabbards were often sewn along the edge of the blade rather than up the centre of the back as on US scabbards.

Imported British sabres were used to some degree, especially the P1853 cavalry sabre; and W. Walsoneid of Solingen, Germany, also made some Confederate swords. Finally, as with every other Confederate necessity, captured US swords were widely used.

In addition, many soldiers brought knives from home. These knives, with blades ranging from 6 ins. to 18 ins. long, were sometimes abandoned later as impractical; but many Southerners, used to carrying knives in civilian life, kept them to the end.

Lances were issued to a number of cavalry units including at least one company of the 5th Virginia Cavalry, several companies of the 4th and 5th Texas Mounted Volunteers, and the 21st, 24th and 25th Texas Cavalry Regiments in early 1862; Col. Joseph O. Shelby's cavalry brigade in south-west Missouri also appear to have had lances in 1862. In February 1861 Gen. Joseph E. Johnston requested lancers armed with 10 ft. ash shafts with a 7 or 8 in. head. The lances he had in his army, he wrote, were poor, 'many of them of heavy wood and too short, the heads too thin and unnecessarily broad'.

The typical Confederate lance appears to have had an 8 ft. ash staff with a 10 in. flat spear point $1\frac{3}{4}$

ins. wide. A pennon of the design of the first Confederate national flag was attached to the staff, and a leather wrist loop was tacked half-way up it; an iron ferrule shod the foot. Lances were largely abandoned by the end of 1862, except by some state defence troops.

The Plates

A1: Private, Infantry, 1861
This man wears the popular overshirt as a jacket. He has a heavy Bowie knive, typically made with a 'D' guard; such knives were commonly brought from home, but many were lost or abandoned as useless weight after only a short time. His musket is a US M1835 flintlock—out of sheer necessity flintlocks remained common until late 1862, even though long obsolete.

A2: Private, 4th Texas Infantry Regiment, 1861
Based on an original photograph of a private in Company H, 4th Texas Infantry Regiment taken in 1861, this man wears a typical 'sack coat'. His waist belt and cartridge box sling are of painted canvas cloth, and he carries a Southern-made tin canteen. His haversack is of the type issued to the US Army during the Mexican–American War of 1846–48. His weapon is a US M1842 smoothbore percussion musket.

A3: First Sergeant, Louisiana Infantry, 1861
Variations of the regulation frock coat were common in 1861. He also wears a white cotton 'havelock' over his cap—generally these were soon abandoned, and used for coffee filters and gun patches. His sword is a Southern-made version of the US Army non-commissioned officer's pattern, and his beltplate is a 'Virginia-style' cast plate. He is armed with an M1841 percussion rifle, commonly called the 'Mississippi Rifle'; these were often rebored to Confederate regulation 0.577 in. calibre. Note black trouser stripe.

B1: Lieutenant-Colonel, Artillery, 1862
Officers generally wore costumes closer to regulation dress than did enlisted men, and caps were also less unusual among commissioned ranks. Note gold trouser welt; and see Plate F1 for jacket cuff button layout. This officer's sabre is a Southern-made copy of the US light artillery officer's model—although cavalry-type sabres were equally, if not more popular than the over-curved light artillery model. The regulation sash worn here would not last long in the field.

The cannon in the background is the 3 in., 10-pdr. 'Parrott rifle', of which numbers were captured from the Union armies; this iron muzzle-loader was the most common rifled piece in Southern service.

Top, **a Cook & Brother artillery musketoon;** *bottom*, **a Cook & Brother cavalry carbine. Close copies of the British Army's issue weapon, the carbine was chosen as the Confederate cavalry's official longarm in 1863. (Russ Pritchard/Milwaukee Public Museum)**

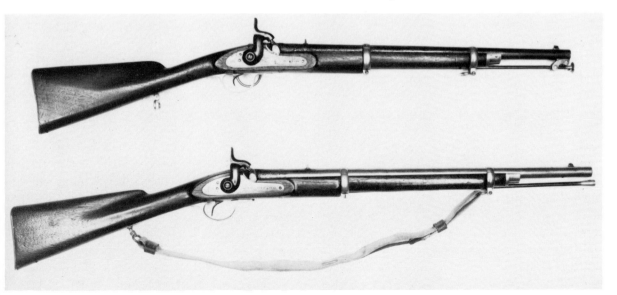

The Southern-made 'Perry' or 'Maynard' carbine. Brass-framed, it is 40 ins. long, with a 21½ in. barrel, and is of 0.52 in. calibre. It was probably made by N. T. Read of Danville, Virginia. (Russ Pritchard)

This 'rising block' carbine is 40¾ ins. long with a 21 in. barrel. Made with all-iron mountings, it is in 0.50 in. calibre. Its maker is unknown. This carbine, like the Morse and Perry, is shown with the breech open. (Russ Pritchard)

The brass-framed, 0.50 in. calibre carbine made by George Morse. It used a metallic cartridge, something rare in the Confederacy, which found it difficult to produce these cartridges. The carbine is 40 ins. long, with a 20 in. barrel. (Russ Pritchard)

The most popular of all Confederate ordnance was the bronze, smoothbore 12-pdr. 'Napoleon' (M1857 gun-howitzer). Despite the rifle's greater range and accuracy, the smoothbore fired faster (having fully fixed ammunition); and at normal battle ranges, especially in wooded country, it was at least as effective as the rifle. The 'Napoleon' was made in many Southern foundries.

B2: Private, Artillery, 1862

For some reason, more photographs show artillery enlisted men in regulation double-breasted frock coats than men from any other branch of service. This man, taken from a photograph of a corporal in the Hanover, Virginia, Artillery varies from the regulations only in that his trousers are grey with a red stripe down each leg. He wears a belt and primer pouch, in which are kept the friction primers used to fire the cannon. His képi is taken from one worn by a member of the Richmond Howitzers and now in the Museum of the Confederacy.

B3: Private, Artillery, 1862

The jacket shown here is taken from one worn in 1864 by a private of the Washington Artillery of New Orleans; note the belt loops on the side, as well as the red trim. He has a US Army gunner's haversack slung over his shoulder. This was used to carry ammunition from the limber chests—which were positioned well behind the cannon in action—so that loose ammunition would not have to be carried exposed.

C1: Captain, Cavalry, 1862

Mounted officers preferred short 'roundabout' jackets to regulation frock coats. The regulation Austrian knot of rank above the cuffs was often not worn. This captain is equipped with an English-made snake buckle; a cap box from the Selma, Alabama, Arsenal and a Southern-made holster, with the pistol butt to the rear, are hidden on his right hip; and a cavalry officer's sabre made by Thomas Griswold & Co., New Orleans. The plumed slouch hat was a common affectation of Confederate cavalrymen.

Since most Southerners were used to riding in civilian life, using English saddles, the adopted regulation military saddle was the 'Jenifer' pattern, seen here. It used an English seat with a military pommel and cantle from which equipment could be suspended, and a surcingle passing through slots in the flaps. It was an easy riding saddle, but it was found to wear on a horse's backbone and withers when the horse grew thinner. It was therefore replaced in the fall of 1863 by the US Army's McClellan saddle. The official saddle blanket was 'dark gray color, with a red border 3 inches wide, 3 inches from the edge. The letters C.S., 6 inches high, of orange color, in the centre of the blanket.' In actual practice, virtually any type of blanket was used. Other horse furniture, such as bridle and bit, was US Army style.

C2: First Lieutenant, Alabama Cavalry, 1862
It was common even until mid-1862 for Confederate officers to use US Army instead of Confederate rank insignia, as worn by this figure based on a photograph of an Alabama cavalry officer. His beltplate is an Alabama issue model, while his sabre was made by L. Haiman & Bro., a Southern company. His cap pouch is English-made, and his holster is similar to the US Army issue type.

C3: Sergeant Major, Cavalry, 1862
Because of their feeling of being an élite force, it appears that cavalrymen tried to obtain yellow material for their facings even though it was uncommon for many other branches of service to wear facing colours. This sergeant major's carbine is a copy of the Enfield type made by Cook & Brother, and his Southern-made copy of the US cavalry sabre was made by C. Hammond.

D1: Private, 2nd Maryland Infantry Regiment, 1863
Pre-war Zouave-style uniforms worn by the Maryland Guard were apparently saved for dress occasions, such as this preparation for a parade in Richmond. The Guard itself served first in a Virginia outfit; then, when Maryland units were raised, they transferred to the 1st Maryland Battalion, most of whose members joined the 2nd Maryland Infantry Regiment when the 1st Battalion was disbanded in 1862. The 2nd Maryland successfully assaulted the Union works on Culp's Hill, near Gettysburg, on 2 July 1863, but were unsuccessful in an attack mounted on the 3rd in conjunction with Pickett's Charge. The regiment lost heavily at Gettysburg, but went on to be commended for its stand at Cold Harbor in 1864.

Two jackets of this style, worn by Maryland Confederates, survived the war and are today in the Museum of the Confederacy. The uniform is a good example of the Southern version of the French Zouave dress. His beltplate is the Maryland version of the stamped brass plate, brought South from its

The Spiller & Burr revolver, with its brass frame and iron cylinder, hammer and barrel. This revolver sometimes came with a detachable shoulder stock. (Russ Pritchard)

Northern maker. Other Confederate Zouave uniforms were similar in design, although details varied from unit to unit.

D2: Bandsman, 1863
This soldier's hat is taken from one in the Museum of the Confederacy, while his waistcoat is in a Mississippi collection. It has small US general service buttons down the woollen front, which has a coarse brown cloth backing; leather wear-strips on the bottom inside edge; and muslin lining. Its back is brown polished cotton, and it has a small belt on the back for size adjustment. The shirt shown here was an imported British Army item dated 1859; the original one was worn by an officer in the 1st Virginia Artillery. This soldier's trousers, taken from a pair worn by a Washington Artillery enlisted man in 1864, are medium-weight charcoal grey wool; the exterior stitching used black thread, while the interior stitching was in white. His band instrument is an over-the-shoulder B flat tenor saxhorn, the most popular type of brass instrument of the period.

D3: Corporal, President's Guard, 1863
The President's Guard was made up of soldiers no longer capable of the physical endeavours needed in the field. It was neatly uniformed. This man's cap and cartridge boxes were apparently made by the same maker, who embossed the letters 'CS' into the outer flaps. His waist belt plate is regulation oval 'CS' model.

E1: Private, Infantry, 1863
The typical Confederate infantryman in the field. His jacket is taken from an original made in North

A copy of the Colt 0.36 in. Navy revolver produced by Griswold & Gunnison. The pistol has a brass frame with a $7\frac{1}{2}$ in. barrel. This particular weapon is a later model with a partly octagonal barrel housing—earlier pistols had rounded housings. (Russ Pritchard)

Carolina and issued to a Maryland soldier; it is lined in white cotton drill, and has two pockets inside the fronts. He is armed with a Richmond Armory version of the M1861 Springfield, and his frame buckle is the 'wishbone' type. His cartridge box is also Richmond-made; its oval copper 'CS' flap plate is hidden here.

E2: Ordnance Sergeant, 28th North Carolina Infantry Regiment, 1863

Photographs indicate that North Carolina ordnance sergeants, whose job was normally to pass out ammunition and to secure abandoned weapons from the battlefield, also carried regimental colours at times. (Usually an ordinary sergeant carried the colour. On 17 February 1864 the Confederate Congress created the rank of 'ensign', who was to wear the insignia of a first lieutenant, and whose duty was to 'bear the colors of the regiment'. Each Confederate regiment carried only one colour.) This NCO carries a version of the Army of Northern Virginia battleflag, adopted in September 1861 as being easier to differentiate from the US national colour on the battlefield. Different sizes were authorised for the different branches of service: 4 ft.-square for infantry, 3 ft.-square for artillery, and $2\frac{1}{2}$ ft.-square for cavalry. (Not all infantry colours were made square, however.) Regiments traditionally painted their battle honours on their colour, a practice officially authorised from 23 July 1862. Here the outer lettering, in straight lines, is (clockwise from top) MANNASSAS/MECHANICS-VILLE/HARPERS FERRY/FRAZIERSFARM; the smaller inner arcs read CEDAR RUN/HANOVER/OX HILL/COLD HARBOR.

The sergeant's cap is a version of the US Army M1839 forage cap; these caps were photographed still being worn by Confederate prisoners as late as 1864. His haversack is captured US Army issue.

E3: Drummer, Infantry, 1863

No special insignia was ordered to be worn by Confederate musicians, nor was there any regulation design for drums. Nevertheless, drums were important both for keeping the beat on the march and for passing on orders in the field and in camp. The white cotton web drum sling was apparently the most common type issued.

F1: Major, Artillery, 1864

Standing near a 24-pdr. gun in a siege battery, this major wears a common variation of the regulation frock coat. His insignia is worn on the lay-down collar, cut in civilian style; note red trouser stripe. He is holding a Southern-made foot artillery sword, the only weapon issued to foot artillerymen for their defence.

F2: Quartermaster Sergeant, Artillery, 1864

This quartermaster sergeant holds the 'guide flag' of the Palmetto Battery from South Carolina. His Southern-made sabre, produced by Hayden & Whilden, is a good copy of the US Army's light artillery sabre. His beltplate is an interesting variation on the standard type, lacking the laurel wreath on the female piece.

F3: Second Lieutenant, Artillery, 1864

This officer wears another common version of the mounted officer's jacket; it is single-breasted, and has the regulation Austrian knot on the sleeves. He also wears the regulation sash, light artillery officer's sabre, and 'chasseur'-pattern képi.

G1: Private, Infantry, 1864

This view shows how the infantryman's accoutrements hang from the rear. His cartridge box was produced by the Houston, Texas, Ordnance Department in 1864, while his canteen is taken from a wooden one carried by an Alabama soldier. His weapon is the Fayetteville Armory rifle, and his haversack is a Southern-made white cotton model.

G2: Sergeant, 4th Kentucky Infantry Regiment, 1864

The Western Confederate armies did not generally use the St Andrew's cross battleflag of the Army o

CONFEDERATE ARTILLERY

The basic unit was the battery, initially of six guns but later usually of four—the shortage of horses was chronic, and as early as mid-1862 the Army of Northern Virginia had significantly more guns than it could take on campaign. The battery was commanded by a captain, and often known by his name (e.g. Carpenter's Battery, Snowden Andrews's Battery, Woolfolk's Battery). Batteries formed in 1861 often took, and kept for some years, locally chosen titles (e.g. the Lynchburg Artillery, Alexandria Artillery, German Artillery, etc.); or names referring to a famous figure (e.g. Jeff Davis Artillery, Pulaski Artillery, etc.).

Two guns, under a lieutenant, formed a section; and one gun, its limber and its caisson formed a platoon, under a sergeant ('chief of piece'). The gun crew was nine men, at full strength; but in a war when smoothbore artillery often went into action within range of riflemen, crew casualties from infantry and counter-battery fire were often murderous, and any passing troops might be pressed into service to help.

The CSA had a motley collection of Southern-made, captured US and imported pieces, and it was not unknown to find three different calibres within one battery—a logistic nightmare. The rifled pieces—e.g. the popular 3 in. Parrott rifle—were more accurate and longer-ranging than the elderly smoothbores like the ubiquitous 12-pdr. Napoleon, but had a marked tendency to bury their shells in the ground before exploding. In broken country, particularly, they were often less effective than the smoothbore, which hardly ever buried its spherical ammunition. Ammunition included solid shot, explosive shell, spherical case (shrapnel), grapeshot and canister.

Until 1863 the CSA dispersed its artillery, one battery per infantry brigade. This robbed them of the concentration of firepower achieved by the Union's massed batteries, e.g. at Malvern Hill. In winter 1862/63 the Army of Northern Virginia began concentrating batteries into battalions (e.g. Longstreet's Corps in April 1865 included Haskell's and Huger's Bns., the latter made up of Moody's, Fickling's, Parker's, Smith's, Taylor's and Woolfolk's Batteries). Even so, it was generally conceded that the Confederate artillery never achieved the level of effectiveness reached by the US Army.

The diagram illustrates three stages of the usual gun drill, which was common to both sides; C = chief of piece, G = gunner:

On the command 'Load':

(1) sponges the barrel; (2) takes a round from (5), who has brought it from the limber in his haversack, and puts it into the muzzle. (1) reverses his ramming staff, and rams it home while (3) covers vent with thumb to prevent airstream igniting unextinguished sparks. (3) then goes to trail and trains piece according to orders of (G), using handspike. (5), alternating with (7), returns to limber for another round; at limber, (6) is cutting fuses—when firing fused ammunition (5) showed fuse to (G) before handing it to (2), to ensure correct interval cut. After laying the piece (G) steps to one side, where he can observe fall of shot, and gives the order

'Ready'

(1) and (2) step clear of recoil; (3) pricks cartridge bag through vent; (4) hooks lanyard to friction-pull primer, and inserts primer in vent. (3) then covers vent with hand to prevent premature discharge, while (4) moves to side and rear, keeping lanyard slack.

'Fire'

(3) steps clear to side, and (4) pulls lanyard. (G) orders gun run forward again, and sequence is repeated. A practised crew could fire two to three rounds a minute.

(Christa Hook)

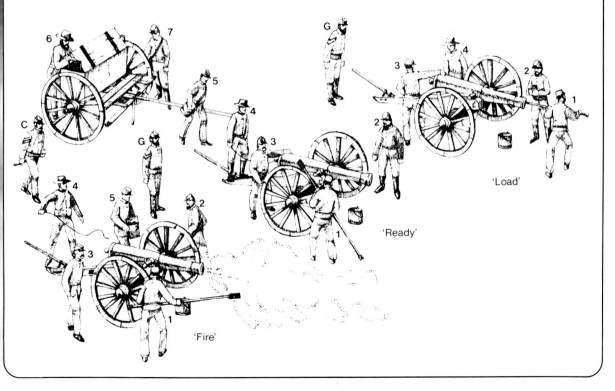

'Load'

'Ready'

'Fire'

Northern Virginia; in their ranks a variety of styles was observed. In Hardee's Division, later Cleburne's Division, the most common colour carried was a variation of this blue and white 'Hardee' flag, which was adopted in mid-1861. The colour was usually smaller than those of the Army of Northern Virginia: that of the 1st Arkansas Infantry was 31 ins. by 38 inches. Battle honours were usually placed on the edge of the flag. This dark blue flag is edged top, bottom and down the 'fly' in white. The battle honours are (*top*) SHILOH·VICKSBURG 1862./(*fly*) BATON ROUGE./(*bottom*) MURFREESBORO·CHICKAMAUGA. The central white disc bears '4.th K.'—all lettering is black. Some of the regiments of Polk's Corps had dark blue colours with a red Greek cross and 11 white stars; and some regiments in the Army of Kentucky appear to have carried colours like that of the 30th Arkansas Infantry, which was 40 ins. by 46 ins., with a blue field bearing a white St Andrew's cross. That particular colour does not have stars now, but may have had them originally. This sergeant's non-commissioned officer's sword was made by Boyle, Gamble & MacFee, one of the largest Southern sword makers. His beltplate is the cast 'CS' type found mostly at Western sites. His regiment is noted for having taken one of the greatest numbers of losses of any Southern unit. The place was the Battle of Shiloh, in which the 4th Kentucky lost 300 killed and 138 wounded.

The identity disc worn by D. W. Snyder, assistant quartermaster of the 56th Virginia Infantry Regiment. The disc (not an issue item—no such discs were ever issued by the Confederates) was made from a silver coin polished smooth on both sides. (Author's collection)

G3: First Lieutenant, 2nd Regiment South Carolina Rifles, 1864

Although Confederate regulations do prescribe a button for riflemen, no other indication of regulation rifle dress is to be found. Nevertheless, rifle buttons were made, and rifle regiments such as this one were organised. Green (not as dark as British rifle green) was the branch-of-service colour in the US Army and militia rifle units, and appears to have been worn by Confederate riflemen as well. Lt. Joseph M. Adams, whose photograph forms the basis for this figure, wore a single-breasted frock with green facings but without the Austrian knots. He is shown here with a Boyle & Gamble Southern-made copy of the US foot officer's sword, and a rare two-piece beltplate with fancy letters and the female piece lacking the usual wreath. Adams was wounded and captured in an unusual night attack made by his regiment against Union forces attempting to relieve Chattanooga on 29 October 1863; he spent the rest of the war as a prisoner.

H1: Private, Infantry, 1865

Some Southern-made overcoats were issued, but they were rare. This figure is taken from a painting by a Confederate veteran. The fur cap and boots were probably obtained from home, as such items do not appear to have been issued to infantrymen. The soldier's buckle is the 'Georgia' frame type, and he has received a British Army cap pouch and cartridge box with his Enfield rifled musket.

H2: Colonel, 44th Georgia Infantry Regiment, 1865

Col. Robert A. Smith of the 44th Georgia was photographed in a plain grey frock coat, with his rank insignia on his standing collar; yet this was not necessarily the regimental norm since other photographs of officers from the same unit show a variety of uniforms, most of them double-breasted. Regardless of dress, however, the 44th were one of the South's toughest regiments; they led the assault at Chancellorsville, driving the Union troops back over two miles and capturing several cannon in the process. They paid a price of 121 officers and men killed, wounded and missing in this action.

The cap badge shown here was taken from the US Army infantry officer's cap badge. Such badges were occasionally worn by Confederate officers, but on the whole were rarer than not. Note sky-blue trouser stripes. His foot officer's sabre was made by Thomas Griswold & Co., New Orleans, one of the best Southern sword makers.

H3: Private, Infantry, 1865

This soldier illustrates to what extent captured US Army uniforms, accoutrements, and weapons were used. If his comrades did not know him, they might well mistake him for a 'blue belly'. His grey cap gives him away, as does the beltplate made by heating a US beltplate until the front fell off and only the frame was left. Otherwise, his cartridge box, cap box, waist belt, haversack, canteen, and M1861 Colt contract rifle musket are all US Army issue items captured and widely used by the Confederates.

Private James J. Dodd, Company C, 4th South Carolina Cavalry Regiment, holds an issue light cavalry sabre. His belt buckle appears to be the most common frame type, and he has a 'Sam Browne'-style sword belt. (Library of Congress)

Select Bibliography

W. A. Albaugh, and E. N. Simmons, *Confederate Arms* (Harrisburg, Pennsylvania, 1957)

W. B. Edwards, *Civil War Guns* (New York, 1962)

W. G. Gavin, *Accoutrement Plates, North & South, 1861–1865* (Philadelphia, 1963)

F. A. Lord, *Civil War Collector's Encyclopedia* (Harrisburg, Pennsylvania, 1963)

C. McCarthy, *Detailed Minutiae of Soldier Life in the Army of Northern Virginia* (Richmond, 1882)

Official, *Regulations for the Army of the Confederate States* (Richmond, 1863)

S. W. Sylvia, and M. J. O'Donnell, *The Illustrated History of Civil War Relics* (Orange, Virginia, 1978)

F. P. Todd, et al, *American Military Equippage, 1851–1872, Volume II* (Providence, Rhode Island, 1977)

Notes sur les planches en couleur

A1 La chemise du genre blouse portée au lieu d'une veste, le couteau et le mousquet à pierre démodé sont typiques des premières années de la guerre. **A2** 'Sack coat' typique; ceintures fabriquées en tissu peint plutôt qu'en cuir; sac à dos de l'armée américaine ancien modèle 1840; mousquet à percussion 1842, à âme lisse plutôt que rayée. **A3** Variation typique de la redingote réglementaire; le revêtement de képi blanc était utilisé dans une certaine mesure au début de la guerre. Le 'fusil Mississippi' 1841 était souvent recalibré au calibre officiel des Confédérés, 0,577 pouce.

B1 L'uniforme réglementaire était plus répandu parmi les officiers que parmi les soldats ordinaires. **B2** L'uniforme de cet homme, appartenant à l'*Hanover Artillery*, en provenance de Virginie, ne diffère de l'uniforme réglementaire que parce que les pantalons sont gris et non bleu clair. **B3** La veste courte, s'arrêtant à la taille, portant souvent des agréments de la couleur du service approprié (infanterie, cavalerie, etc) était plus répandue que la redingote réglementaire.

C1 La veste courte, souvent dépourvue des noeuds de passementerie réglementaires au-dessus des manchettes, était portée de façon presque universelle par la cavalerie. Le chapeau à plume et à larges bords était une mode souvent adoptée. **C2** Les épaulettes de grade de l'armée américaine se rencontraient chez les officiers confédérés en 1861–62. L'équipement en cuir était soit importé—souvent d'Angleterre—soit fabriqué localement, généralement en cuir brun. **C3** Des parements de couleur—ici, le jaune de la cavalerie—étaient plus souvent rencontrés dans la cavalerie que dans d'autres services, qui limitaient généralement les détails décoratifs à des liserés de la couleur appropriée. La carabine est une copie locale de l'*Enfield*.

D1 Exemple typique d'un uniforme confédéré de style 'zouave', d'après un spécimen parvenu jusqu'à nous. **D2** Il est probable que de nombreux confédérés portaient ce type de costume totalement civil. **D3** Uniforme exceptionnellement élégant, porté par cette unité de gardes du corps recrutés parmi des hommes à la forme physique insuffisante pour le combat.

E1 Fantassin sudiste typique des années du milieu de la guerre, d'après des exemples encore existants d'uniformes et d'équipements. Le mousquet à âme rayée est une copie fabriquée à *Richmond* du *Springfield* 1861. **E2** Une caractéristique des unités de *North Carolina* était que l'*ordnance sergeant* portait le drapeau du régiment, en plus de ses devoirs relatifs aux canons et aux munitions. Le képi est une copie du type 1839 américain, encore porté sur des photos jusqu'en 1864. **E3** Il n'y avait pas de réglements sur l'uniforme exact des tambours ou sur le modèle de leur instrument.

F1 Variation de la redingote d'officier, de style civil, avec col ouvert. **F2** Le *quartermaster sergeant* tient le 'guide flag' de la *Palmetto Battery*, unité de South Carolina. **F3** Une autre version répandue de la veste portée par les officiers montés, ici avec les noeuds de passementerie réglementaires sur les manches; képi de style 'Chasseur'.

G1 Agencement arrière de l'équipement du fantassin; tous les articles sont tirés d'exemples encore existants de l'équipement fabriqué dans le sud. **G2** Le drapeau de cette unité est typique des modèles plus petits et plus variés portés par les régiments des armées de l'ouest de la Confédération, où le modèle à croix de St André ('stars and bars') n'était pas souvent rencontré. Le 4th Kentucky eut 438 morts ou blessés à la bataille de Shiloh. **G3** Une photo de Lt. Joseph Adams a inspiré ce tableau; Les Uniformes de 'rifle regiment' à parements verts étaient rares mais existaient dans les deux armées.

H1 Rare paletot de fabrication par les confédérés et équipement principalement anglais, porté par un personnage inspiré par un tableau peint par un confédéré vétéran. **H2** D'après une photo de Col. Robert Smith, qui mena ce régiment distingué dans l'attaque de Chancellorsville où ils firent reculer l'ennemi de deux miles; Uniforme simple, assez conforme aux réglements. **H3** A part le képi gris, cet homme est presque totalement vêtu d'éléments de l'armée américaine pris durant le combat.

Farbtafeln

A1 Typisch für die frühen Kriegsjahre sind das kittelartige Hemd anstelle der Jacke, das Messer und eine altmodische Steinschlossmuskete. **A2** Typischer 'sack coat'; Gürtel aus bemaltem Stoff statt Leder: US Army Tornister von 1840; Perkussionsmuskete von 1842 mit glattgebohrtem Lauf statt Stutzen. **A3** Typische Variation des regulären Uniformrocks; die weisse Kappenbedeckung wurde zem Teil schon zu Anfang des Krieges getragen. Der 'Mississippi-Stutzen' von 1841 wurde häufig auf das offizielle Kaliber der Konföderierten neu gebohrt (0,577 in).

B1 Die reguläre Uniform war häufiger bei bestallten als bei gewöhnlicher Soldaten anzutreffen. **B2** Diese Uniform eines Mitglieds der *Hanover Artillery* aus Virginia unterscheidet sich von der regulären nur durch die grauen anstelle der hellblauen Hosen. **B3** Die kurze Jacke mit Hüftlänge, häufig mit den Farben der entsprechenden Waffengattung besetzt (Infanterie, Kavallerie usw.), war weiter verbreitet als der reguläre Rockmantel.

C1 Die kurze Jacke (manchmal ohne die regulären Tressenknoten über den Manschetten) wurde fast überall von den Kavalleristen getragen. Der Federhut mit breiter Krempe war eine häufige Affektation. **C2** 1861/62 sah man unter den Offizieren der Konföderierten Staaten häufig Schulterrangstreifen der US Army Die Lederausrüstung war entweder importiert (oft aus England) oder im Land selbst hergestellt, meist aus braunem Leder. **C3** Farbflächen (hier das Gelb der Kavallerie) waren in der Kavallerie häufiger als in anderen Waffengattungen, die den Uniformschmuck gewöhnlich auf Schnurbesatz in den entsprechender Farben beschränkte. Der Karabiner ist eine amerikanische Kopie einer *Enfield*.

D1 Ein typisches Beispiel für den 'Zouave' Stil der Konfödierten-Uniform, nach einem erhalten gebliebenen Exemplar. **D2** Viele Konföderierte truger wahrscheinlich diese ganz zivile Bekleidung. **D3** Eine ungewöhnlich elegante Uniform, von dieser Leibwacheneinheit getragen, deren Mitglieder nicht mehr für Kampfeinsätze geeignet waren.

E1 Typischer südlicher Infanterist aus der Mitte des Krieges, nach erhalter gebliebenen Exemplaren der Uniform und Ausrüstung. Die Stutzermuskete is eine 1861 von *Richmond* hergestellte Kopie einer *Springfield*. **E2** Bei den Einheiter aus *North Carolina* war es üblich, dass der *ordnance sergeant* die regimentsflagge trug zusätzlich zu seiner Verantwortung für Gewehre und Munition. Die Kappe ist eine Kopie des 1839 von den US getragenen Modells, das noch in späten Foto: aus dem Jahr 1864 zu sehen ist. **E3** Es gab keine Vorschriften für die Uniformer von Trommlern oder für den Entwurf von Trommeln.

F1 Variation des Uniformmantels eines Offiziers, im zivilen Stil, mit offenen Kragen. **F2** Der *quartermaster sergeant* hält die 'guide flag' der *Palmetto Battery*, Einheit aus South Carolina. **F3** Eine andere häufige Version der von berittener Offizieren getragenen Jacke, hier mit regulären Tressenknoten auf den Ärmeln dazu ein Käpi im 'Chasseur' Stil.

G1 Hintere Anordnung der Ausrüstung eines Infanteristen; alle Gegenstände nach erhalten gebliebenen Exemplaren einer im Süden hergestellten Ausrüstung **G2** Die Flagge dieser Einheit ist typisch für die kleineren und mannigfaltigerer Regimentsabzeichen der westlichen Konföderierten Staaten wo das Andreas kreuz ('stars and bars') gewöhnlich nicht auftrat. Das 4th Kentucky hatte bei der Schlacht von Shiloh 438 Toten und Verletzte. **G3** Ein Foto von Lt. Joseph Adam war die Grundlage für dieses Gemälde; grüne 'rifle regiment' Uniformen warer selten, aber in beiden Armeen gelegentlich vertreten.

H1 Seltener, von den Konföderierten hergestellter Mantel, weitgehend englisch Ausrüstung, von einer Gestalt getragen, die aus dem Gemälde eine Konföderierten-Veteranen übernommen wurde. **H2** Nach einem Foto von Col Robert Smith, der dieses bedeutende Regiment im Angriff von Chancellorsvill führte, als der Feind zwei Meilen weit zurückgeschlagen wurde; eine einfache Uniform, eng an die Reulationen angelehnt. **H3** Abgesehen von der grauer Kappe ist dieser Mann durchgehend mit erbeuteten Gegenständen der US Army ausgestattet.